"How could a book be _____
vational all at the same _____
reality in *Keep the Door*_____
ing and finished by dinnertime. I couldn't put it down, and frankly,
that rarely happens for me. Thank you, Kristin, for this beautiful
contribution. It is a must-have for those considering becoming foster and adoptive parents."

—**Sherrie Eldridge**, author of *Twenty Things Adopted
Kids Wish Their Adoptive Parents Knew*

"Kristin Berry has written an honest, hope-filled book about the joys
and heartbreak of foster care. *Keep the Doors Open* offers a transparent look into her life as a foster mom—she doesn't hold back
about the challenges or the wonder of caring for children in desperate need. You'll love her for the way she nurtures the children who
come through her door and for her sorrow when they leave. *Keep
the Doors Open* may light a fire in your soul to say yes to fostering a
child for the first time or to keeping your own doors and heart open
to the next child needing a safe place to land."

—**Lisa Qualls**, author, speaker, and creator of
the *One Thankful Mom* blog

"Kristin Berry is a master storyteller. *Keep the Doors Open* poignantly
weaves the tale of a family's journey through foster care and adoption. More than that, it serves as a window into the heart of a mother.
Kristin shares her family's story with grace and compassion, wit and
wisdom. I could not put this book down and found strength, inspi-
ration, and direction in its pages."

—**Jamie C Finn**, creator of the *Foster the Family* blog
and *Real Mom* podcast

Keep the Doors Open

KRISTIN BERRY

HARVEST HOUSE PUBLISHERS
EUGENE, OREGON

Cover design by Kara Klontz Design

Cover photo © Alexandre Zveiger, Tr1sha, Africa Studio, Patricia Hofmeester, P Maxwell Photography, Lora liu, JIANG HONGYAN, Fedorovekb, John Andrus / shutterstock

This book includes stories in which people's names and some details of their situations have been changed to protect their privacy.

Keep the Doors Open
Copyright © 2019 by Kristin Berry
Published by Harvest House Publishers
Eugene, Oregon 97408
www.harvesthousepublishers.com

ISBN 978-0-7369-7669-5 (pbk)
ISBN 978-0-7369-7670-1 (eBook)

Library of Congress Cataloging-in-Publication Data

Names: Berry, Kristin, author.
Title: Keep the doors open : lessons learned from a year of foster
    parenting / Kristin Berry.
Description: Eugene, Oregon : Harvest House Publishers, [2019]
Identifiers: LCCN 2019022552 (print) | LCCN 2019022553 (ebook) | ISBN
    9780736976695 (paperback) | ISBN 9780736976701 (ebook)
Subjects: LCSH: Berry, Kristin. | Foster parents--United States. | Foster
    children--United States. | Parenting--United States.
Classification: LCC HQ759.7 .B469 2020 (print) | LCC HQ759.7 (ebook) |
    DDC 306.874--dc23
LC record available at https://lccn.loc.gov/2019022552
LC ebook record available at https://lccn.loc.gov/2019022553

Printed in the United States of America
                19 20 21 22 23 24 25 26 27 / VP-GL / 10 9 8 7 6 5 4 3 2 1

Dear Reader,

When you think of the foster care system, what comes to mind? Do you imagine overworked caseworkers and tired caregivers, scared kids and discouraged birth parents? Yes, it's all of that.

Do you also feel the quiet stirring of a passion deep within you? Do you wonder what it would be like to do something daring or maybe a little risky? What if you opened your vulnerable heart to help others? Have you ever pondered the path of foster care and wondered if it was time for you to venture in a new direction?

Mike and I faced these questions and fears when we considered becoming foster parents 16 years ago. We decided to go for it, knowing that it would be difficult—and it was. In fact, after several years of foster parenting and many bumps in the road, we considered closing our license.

After months of wrestling with our decision, we realized we just weren't ready to give up. We made a commitment to open our doors to whomever needed us for one more year. We faced that year with a thrilling sense of stepping into the unknown. Opening our doors to help others felt both terrifying and exciting. We learned that opening our doors to those in need often forced us to come face to face with our own weakness. We learned not only to welcome others but to allow ourselves to be loved as well.

This book is a compilation of stories from our nine years as foster parents. As you read these stories, I hope that you too will face your calling and the future with an openness that changes the world around you.

Wishing you adventure,

Kristin

CONTENTS

Part 1

THE SEASON
BEFORE

1

THE INVITATION
TO ENTER

I closed my eyes and tried to remember the beginning. The memory is kept so far back that it's hard to grasp. With my lids pressed together, I reached further than I thought possible, and then, there it was. The first memory of my grandfather. Yes, that is where my story begins.

My grandfather was the tallest man I had ever known. At least that's how it seemed from where I stood. I craned my neck to look up at his soft white hair. He grinned down at me from his favorite rocking chair. "How are you, tweetie?" he asked in a soft voice. I crinkled my nose at the mispronounced word and reached my arms up to him. I crawled onto his lap and waited for him to turn his hearing aid down. His red cardigan smelled like soap and Old Spice.

"It's 'sweetie,' Grandpa," I corrected him gently.

"Oh, I know, I know. It's just that my tongue doesn't say it quite right."

I raised myself up onto my knees and looked him square in the eyes. "Show me your tongue again, Grandpa," I requested with unashamed curiosity. He smiled again and stuck his tongue out for me to examine. Just below the tip of his tongue, a bite-size piece was missing.

"When I was littler than you, someone wasn't holding on tight enough. They dropped me, and I almost bit it right off." He paused for effect. "At the hospital, the doctor wanted to remove the whole thing, but my mom wouldn't let that happen, so they did their best to fix me up." And with that, he lowered me to the floor, patted me on the head, and returned his focus to *Wheel of Fortune*.

When I was in early elementary school, I overheard my grandfather talking about his plan to meet his biological siblings for the first time. The adults were standing around the kitchen table long after the Thanksgiving dinner had ended. My grandmother was wiping the counter down, and my aunts were drying the silverware. My mom and dad were returning chairs and tables to storage, and I was supposed to be folding the tablecloth. The steady dance of cleaning, folding, and putting away stopped abruptly. I was keenly aware that this was not a conversation for me, and yet I inched closer, straining to hear. I tucked the half-folded tablecloth under one arm and braced myself against the doorframe so I could lean in just a little closer. I couldn't understand how my grandpa had never met his own brothers and sisters. At the moment, mine were chasing one another relentlessly through the basement playroom with several of my cousins. They were making it difficult to eavesdrop, but nevertheless, as I tried to imagine not knowing them, my heart filled with a sense of vast emptiness.

Once the dishes were done and the house was returned to order, my parents called us to the car, and we hugged all the relatives goodbye. My mom reminded us to buckle up and then turned the radio to Christmas music. I smiled as I thought about how much I loved the Christmas season and our traditions as a family. My brother fell asleep with his head on my shoulder, and my sister softly sang along with the music. I listened to the even tone of my parents' conversation. I couldn't make out the words, but I loved the soothing sound of their voices. Love filled my heart, and I felt like I might burst with affection for my family. My eyes drifted shut, and I began to daydream about Christmas morning.

"Wait!" My eyes shot open as I looked directly at my startled parents. "What happened to Grandpa's brothers and sisters? Why doesn't he know them? Is he going to meet them?"

My dad drew in a breath before reminding me that eavesdropping is rude. Then he told me a little about my grandfather's story. "Grandpa lived in a lot of foster homes when he was a kid, but his brothers and sisters were adopted by another family. They have never met, but they just reached out to your grandpa, and they would all like to get to know one another."

I pondered this for a moment and then replied, "What's a foster home?"

My dad closed his eyes for just a moment, and I could see the words roll around on his tongue before he spoke them. "Sometimes a family can't take care of a child, and a foster family takes care of the child for a while. Your grandpa's family couldn't take care of him, so he lived in a few foster homes. But they didn't take good care of him either."

I let that sink in for a while as I watched the snow swirl outside my window. My baby brother's hot breath against my shoulder reminded me of a question that had plagued me for years. "What really happened to Grandpa's tongue?"

My dad shook his head, and my mom gave him a warning glance toward the back seat. "I don't know," my dad finally responded. I didn't ask again.

I was 12 when my parents started talking about adoption in our own family. I was listening to their conversation from the top of the stairs long after I had been sent to bed. Next to reading by the night-light, eavesdropping was my favorite late-night pastime. (I realize as I type this that I owe my parents an apology for never going right to bed and for listening to all kinds of conversations and television programs that were none of my business. I also fully accept that I deserve the nosy children that currently reside in my own home.)

That night I strained my ears to hear each detail. They had been watching a television program about children who had been left in orphanages in Romania. I could tell from their hushed tones that they were horrified by the conditions and the lack of resources many of these places had to care for children. They talked late into that night about the mothers who must be devastated to leave their children there but felt they had no other option. They wondered out loud how this could be happening when families like ours had plenty of room in our homes, more than enough resources, and certainly an abundance of love to give. I don't know if they talked about my grandpa, but I tucked my knees beneath my nightgown and imagined him as a child with nowhere to go and no one to tuck him in at night. A seed was planted in my own heart as I imagined my possible brother in one of those orphanages right at that moment. I wondered if he had enough to eat. I wondered if he was cold. I crept back to my bed and knelt next to it in prayer for this unknown child before I slipped between the covers.

My grandfather died when I was 16. He was diagnosed with stomach cancer and had been admitted to the hospital for surgery. I visited him the day before he passed away. I found a small stuffed lamb with a pink bow tied around its neck and brought it to him. I honestly have no idea why I chose it. I wish it had some deeper meaning. That giant man lay beneath the crisp white hospital sheet with his head propped up on a pillow. Tufts of white stood on end, escaping from his carefully combed hair. I resisted the urge to reach out and smooth them down. I set the lamb on the tray next to his bed and felt a little silly to be bringing a stuffed animal to a grown man.

He patted my arm. "Thank you, tweetie. I love it." I hugged his neck and breathed in the same scent of soap and Old Spice I knew from my childhood. Family members milled around, talking, whispering, waiting. I perched on the back of the plastic couch next to the window and pressed my forehead to the cool glass. I spotted our van parked below and the trees budding in the brisk April air. Soon it was time to leave, and I felt confident my grandfather would be home shortly as I kissed his cheek goodbye.

The following day, my mom picked me up early from school so I could take my driver's test. I slid into the front seat of our Caprice Classic excitedly, but when I looked at her face, I knew something was wrong.

"Grandpa died today," she told me gently. "He had a heart attack on his way to surgery."

We didn't talk as we drove to the Bureau of Motor Vehicles. My heart felt numb, and I took the test despite the feeling of grief welling up inside of me. I failed. I got back into the car with my mother, and she started driving to my grandmother's house. Then I burst into tears. I wanted to ask him more questions. I wanted to know him better. I wanted to tell him that whatever bad things had happened to him, I was proud and thankful to be his granddaughter. It was too late.

I learned a little more about who this man was in the days that followed. My family sorted through his belongings, and each item sparked a story. I listened as they shared memories of the dad and grandpa I knew and silently filed away stories I'd never heard before. I tried to reconcile multiple foster homes, abuse, neglect, rejection, misunderstandings, and anger with the gentle and unshakable grandpa I knew. My grandfather did not let the actions of others define him, that much was clear.

His funeral was a testament to his resilience and perseverance. The viewing lasted for hours as people lined up out the door and around the block to pay their respects. My cousins and I shook hands, hugged, got bored, wandered up and down the sidewalk, and returned to shake hands and hug some more. As we said our final farewell at the cemetery, I wiped the tears from my cheeks and pulled my jacket a little tighter around my shoulders. We filed slowly back to the car, and I glanced up at my father, who had just become fatherless. I wanted to see if he looked different. I wondered about the man we buried, who had been without a father most of his life. Deep in my soul, an idea began to sprout. There would be another child who needed a home in the future, and I would open my door. I felt that in my heart with certainty.

Three months after my grandfather passed away, my parents traveled to Bulgaria to bring my brother home. They had been in the process of adopting for almost four years, and the location had changed from Romania to Bulgaria as Romania closed its doors to international adoption. My grandma came to stay us while my parents were away. I went to the library and checked out a book about Bulgaria that was filled with statistics and grainy pictures. (Oh, the things we used to do before the internet.) I squinted at the pictures, moving them in and out of focus as I tried to picture my brother growing up in this country so far away. We had a snapshot of him attached to the refrigerator. In the picture, he looked much smaller than a typical eight-year-old child, but it was hard for me to judge. His hair was shiny and black and fell stick-straight across his forehead. His head was tilted to one side with his good eye peering curiously at the camera and the other wandering aimlessly. I touched the photograph and imagined what it would be like to hug him.

In the room that would soon be his, I ran my fingers along the edge of the quilt my mother had made for him. The quilt was made from a brightly colored fabric map of the world. My mom had sewed it together and stitched along the outline of Bulgaria and the United States. I loved him already and counted down the days until I would become a big sister to a new sibling once again.

The years that followed were at times confusing. I hadn't realized that I wouldn't be able to talk to him when he arrived. I know that sounds ignorant, and I suppose it was. I knew he had a different language and even a different alphabet, but I was so excited to meet him that I didn't think it would matter. One of my good friends was Bulgarian by birth, and she tried to help me learn some Bulgarian.

My parents took us to an adoption support group with other adoptive families. My brother had a few people he could talk to, but in the end, he stopped trying to speak to us in his native tongue and eventually took ours. I know my parents felt sad that he lost that part of himself. I imagine he did too. Even though our family dynamic changed, I felt like he was our missing piece. I found it hard to remember a time when I didn't have him as a brother.

At 19 years old, I had the opportunity to go to Jamaica during spring break. A team of students from my college was going there to learn about the culture and participate in some activities intended to help the community we were visiting. While I was there, I visited an orphanage in the mountains of Mandeville. The trip up the mountain was a diversion from our original plan. We were supposed to be painting classrooms at a local school, but lines had been crossed, and the supplies we needed were not available.

We traveled in a 15-passenger van, and I soon discovered that it was not customary for passengers to wear seat belts. At first, I didn't buckle mine, but as the van sped faster and faster toward our destination without regard for the cliffs that dropped sharply right outside the cracked windows, I succumbed to the limited protection the lap belt would provide. After an hour, the bare skin of my legs stuck sharply to the hot vinyl seat. Pools of sweat gathered behind my knees, and I longed to stick my head out of the open passenger window like my family's pet border collie.

After four hours, we finally slowed, and the driver pressed the turn signal. The rhythmic ticking cut through the silence that had filled the space between us weary travelers. A large chain-link gate opened as we approached our destination. I spotted four white-washed buildings with sharp green roofs. The property was tidy and simple. Little girls in matching gingham dresses played in the yard, and little boys in tan pants and white shirts rode bikes and pulled wagons. The children parted to allow the van to pass.

Before I left the country, I made plans to return to the orphan-age as a volunteer the following autumn. I spent that summer work-ing two jobs to save money for my trip. One was detailing cars, and the other was at a tiny bookstore on the main street of my home-town. One day when I went in to start my shift at the bookstore, I noticed an envelope with my name on it tucked under the cash reg-ister. I looked around to see if someone had recently left it. I asked my boss about it, and she grinned and shook her head. "I don't know who could have done something like that!" I had a suspicion that she knew exactly who had left it there. I opened the envelope to find a simple note written in neat cursive. "I hope you have a won-derful trip this fall. I have no doubt you will do great things." No signature. I turned the card over and parted the envelope to put it back. Inside was a check for the exact amount I had left to raise for my plane ticket.

I spent those few months teaching preschool, washing dishes, and hanging laundry. It turned out the things I was good at were nei-ther great nor memorable. I was good at the mundane, the routine, and the forgotten things. I enjoyed the solitude of mending school uniforms that would be torn again by spring and the cool breeze against my skin as sheets and towels bustled in the crisp morning air.

I had just found my groove with these daily tasks when the dorm mom for the girls' dorm left. As a 19-year-old American college student, I reluctantly stepped into a role I knew I was not qualified for. I loved it. I added new activities to my routine: nighttime stories, prayers, and tying shoes and hair ribbons before breakfast.

A nine-year-old named Zindzey tormented me with everything she had in her. She poked fun at my hair, my freckles, my accent, and even the way I walked. I physically bit my own tongue to prevent it from releasing the string of words I was in danger of assaulting her with at any moment.

One night, I had just switched off my light and curled up under my thin, worn blanket when I heard a cry from the little girls' room. I jumped to my feet and ran into the room, searching the rows of beds for the screaming child. When my hand finally landed on the fitful girl, I realized it was Zindzey. I crouched next to her and placed my hand on her now sweating forehead. She whimpered, "No, no, no, don't leave me, don't leave me, Mommy."

I sat with her long into the night, my fingers smoothing her soft hair. In the glow of the night-light, I marveled at the silver wisps of one section of hair near her forehead. They were like an ornament, a beautiful decoration. I tucked them back into her beautiful black braids with my pinky finger and stroked her forehead until her breathing slowed and she slipped back into sleep. As I sat there, I wondered about the mommy who couldn't be there, and I cried. I returned home the following Christmas and knew that my purpose was forever changed.

2

OPENING THE DOORS

I met Mike just four weeks before my twentieth birthday. I was standing in the lobby of his dorm, waiting on some friends to go dancing. We went to a very conservative college, and dancing wasn't allowed, so I'm sure we used some sort of code phrase—"going to get coffee" or something like that. I had been home from Jamaica for a month and wasn't sure how to process the difference between that culture's poverty and my own's excess.

I had sworn off dating, but I saw Mike from across the room and liked his casual confidence. He walked toward me and nodded at my friends. He stuck his hand out to shake mine and introduced himself. I pretended to be indifferent. On a college campus of approximately 1,500, I already knew his name, but I liked that he made the effort. The following week, I noticed he was in a few of my classes and made sure to sit in front of him and pretend not to notice he was there. He says there was a lot of hair flipping involved; I can neither confirm nor deny this. He waited for me after class one day and asked me on a date. I said yes and spent the rest of the week looking forward to seeing him again.

It was on an icy winter night in February. Classes had been canceled for a week, and I was kind of worried that our date wouldn't go as planned. He drove a royal-blue Firebird that was equal parts redneck and cool—and 100 percent impractical for the snow-covered hills of Cincinnati. He picked me up at five, and we weaved our way down the hills toward the Ohio River, where we ate dinner at a floating restaurant. I was always a little nervous at those places out on the water, but I didn't want to ruin his plan, so I kept my fear to myself. We were seated at a table by the window where we could watch the barges float past. The sun was quickly setting, and before I knew it, we were so involved in conversation, I had forgotten my terrifying certainty that we were going to plunge into the icy Ohio River and die a cold, slow, hypothermic death. We left the restaurant and decided to go for coffee. He was honest and straightforward, and it was a relief to spend time with someone who didn't seem to be putting on a front. I didn't want the date to end.

We slipped and slid our way back up into the hills surround-ing the city, and he parallel parked in front of one of my favor-ite coffee shops. (I was impressed by the parallel parking, which is why I mention it here.) We stayed and talked long enough for the snowplows to make their way down the street once again. By the time we returned to the car, it was completely buried in snow on all sides. I suppressed a grin while Mike tried to assess the situation. He remained a gentleman, opening the passenger door for me and starting the car for warmth. I thanked him and watched as he dug out the tires with the window scraper. I peered in the rearview mir-ror as he reached the back tire, which was encased in a large piece of ice. He kicked it and muttered in frustration under his breath.

We went to college with young men and women destined to "do great things for the kingdom of God." What they meant was min-istry in the church, and "real ministry" did not include getting frus-trated and kicking the tire of a frozen car. I laughed out loud when I saw him. He caught my eye and smiled sheepishly back. The ice came loose, and he slid cautiously into the driver's seat. "Um, sorry I lost my cool."

"That's okay," I responded. "That was the most honest thing I've seen in a long time. Plus, getting stuck just makes this night a bigger adventure."

We went out again a week later, this time to a comedy program. I had been sick with a cold all week and had completely lost my voice. I was looking forward to spending time with Mike and didn't want to miss a minute, so I bundled myself up and shoved tissues in each pocket. We belly laughed the whole night, though I really made more of a croaking sound. My bright-red nose, missing voice, and endless need for tissues didn't scare him off, and to my surprise, he asked me out again the following week. We planned to go for a walk in the local park.

The walk led to lunch out, which led to studying together at the library, which led to dinner. As we drove to the restaurant, his car made a horrible sound, and then we heard a crash. He looked in the rearview mirror and started to laugh. "My muffler just fell off!" I laughed too. We couldn't seem to spend time together without some sort of mishap. I loved it. I felt free to be myself, and I think he did too. From the muffler on, we were an item. We talked about everything and argued about even more. I loved that I could have an opinion and be heard. He was willing to question life right alongside me and not be intimidated by the hard questions I asked of the world around me or of the life I wanted to lead.

One day, I told him about my plan to adopt. I said it casually and without much thought. I had been raised with stories of adoption and foster care, and the idea came naturally to me.

Mike froze midsentence. "Wait, what?"

I paused too. "I really want to adopt my children. I think I'd like to be a foster parent or maybe even move back to Jamaica to work in the children's home." The silence around us thickened until it was almost difficult to breathe.

Finally, he said, "I always pictured myself working in a church in the suburbs, raising two kids who look like me…you know, just the usual." I was shocked—it wasn't at all what I pictured for myself, and I didn't know how to proceed. Mike squeezed my hand. "Oh well, we've only been dating a few months. Who knows where we'll end up?"

I squeezed his hand back. "Fair enough."

We got married the following year and began working at a little church in the suburbs of Cincinnati. I gave up my ministry at the church in the city but soon filled my time with mentoring children at our church. To my surprise, I loved teaching junior high kids. I found them delightfully quirky and enthusiastic. Mike and I weren't ready for kids yet, so I decided not to push the issue of adoption. Over the years, it came up naturally as we talked about our future. Mike met a few friends who were adoptive dads, and his heart became soft to the idea. He asked honest questions of his friends and received helpful answers. The day he came to me and told me he had been thinking a lot about adoption, I was shocked. I thought about children all the time, but I hadn't wanted to be pushy. We called a local adoption agency and went to an information meeting the following month.

After three years of marriage, we adopted our first daughter. Grace was breathtakingly beautiful. Her arrival was celebrated by grandparents, aunts, uncles, church members, and neighbors. My youngest brother was especially interested in her and asked many questions about her adoption. Her arrival opened the door for my brother and me to talk about his own adoption story.

Our daughter was two years old when one of my friends asked if I could take her children for just a little while—maybe a few weeks—so she could get things in order. We found out that we needed a foster license and scrambled to get the paperwork done.

Early that summer, we brought my friend's children, Christine and Aaron, into our home—our first foster placement. We were completely unprepared. We had received 20 hours of training through our local DCS (Department of Child Services) but quickly found we were lacking the skills to complete everyday tasks, including processing WIC (Women, Infants, and Children) checks or enrolling in a Head Start preschool program.

We discovered early on that the caseworker assigned to the children was completely swamped with cases and took days or even weeks to return calls. This posed a significant problem when we needed to take a child to the doctor or obtain the address of the visitation center we were required to be at in an hour. We became resourceful in every way. I learned to push for information at doctors' offices and found out I could stand for hours in the DCS lobby with a one-, two-, and three-year-old until someone located a child's birth certificate or Social Security number. I bit my tongue when the lady from Family and Social Services talked slowly to me, as if receiving food stamps had somehow stripped me of my college degree.

I didn't really think of myself as a foster parent at first. I was only doing this for a friend. I was certain that the children would be living with her again soon. I felt a kinship with my friend and was certain I would want someone to do this for me if I ever needed help. Three years went by while my friend took two steps forward and three steps back. Within that time, she gave birth to two more children and lost them to the foster-care system as well.

We adopted Christine and Aaron four years after they came to live with us. We were officially a family of five when we walked out of the courtroom into the crisp spring air. We had never intended to foster or to adopt from the foster-care system. We had seemingly stumbled into a culture and way of life that we hadn't previously known existed. And we knew there were other children in need of temporary homes.

The families we encountered in our four years as foster parents changed the way we saw the world around us. We met good foster parents who loved unconditionally and strived to parent a never-ending stream of children in a way that would celebrate each child's uniqueness and foster positive identity. We saw birth parents who fought with everything within them to escape poverty, drug addiction, and homelessness. Sadly, we also witnessed foster parents who didn't treat children or families with the dignity that every human deserves. That was the thing that stuck with us the most.

As we left that courthouse, we had a decision to make—to close our license or open our heart to the next family who needed a little support. We kept our license up to date but told our case manager we needed a little break. During that break, Mike and I were honest with one another about the ups and downs of foster care. We both admitted that we felt like we had been run ragged during the past four years.

Now that we weren't foster parents, we felt immense freedom. Freedom to visit family four hours away without getting permission from a judge to cross state lines. Freedom from endless court hearings and surprise visits from social workers. Freedom from feeling constantly judged. Freedom from having to defend our choice of pediatrician, school, or even brand of car seat. We realized we needed the break more than we had known. But we also knew that the family we dreamed of was larger than just the five of us. We decided to keep our license on hold and pursue another private adoption.

We went back to the adoption agency we used with Christine. We loved the staff and the environment of the agency. It felt good to be there, but even now, I can look back on the feeling of unease that settled over us at that time. I couldn't stop thinking of the families who were caught up in the foster-care system. I imagined the children who needed a place to stay and the parents who just needed a chance.

But I desperately wanted to hold another baby in my arms and to call that baby my own. My imagination went to baby names and decorating a nursery. Over the next few months, we completed our profile and began to meet birth moms who came looking for a family. We were matched a couple of times, but the birth mom always changed her mind. We felt confident that we would be matched with the right person, so we waited patiently.

Finally, we met a birth mom who seemed certain that we were the right choice for her. We paid for our home study, fingerprints, background checks, and physicals. We saved up money for our attorney and the birth mother's living expenses. She met us for lunch and brought the ultrasound pictures with her. She surprised us by telling us that it was a girl. As the date drew near, we made the crib up with pink sheets printed with delicate white roses. My sister sent us the tiniest ballerina slippers I'd ever seen. I displayed them on the nightstand next to an intricate antique lamp and the rocking chair where I had rocked all my children.

We talked with the birth mom a few times a week, and she even talked with Christine and Grace on the phone. I felt like it might be a little risky to let the kids know so much about her in case she changed her mind, but I also thought it was important for the mom to know that her little daughter would have such wonderful big sisters.

One night, we took the kids to swim lessons at the high school swimming pool. It was freezing outside, and the kids were thrilled to get to swim in the heated pool. The phone rang while I watched them swim. I answered it, but the room was crowded and loud. It was the adoption counselor—I strained to hear the details. Birth mom was in the hospital with complications. She told us it was okay to message her but that she might not get back. I did and told her that we were praying for her safety. She was released a few days later and put on strict bed rest. I worried about her, but things seemed to be fine. We continued to plan for the new baby and prepare the kids and our home for her arrival.

One day, the birth mom didn't answer my call. I wasn't worried. I didn't hear back for the rest of the week, but I didn't call because I didn't want her to think I was being pushy. I backed off entirely. The following week, the adoption counselor called and said they had lost complete contact with the birth mother. I wasn't surprised, but I was very sad.

I waited for weeks for her to call and tell me something. She didn't. I allowed myself to call one time and made a plan that it would be the only call. I paced around my bedroom, working up the nerve. Finally, I took the tiny ballet slippers into my hand and climbed into my closet. I shut the door behind me and curled into a ball on the floor beneath Mike's jackets. When I dialed the number, it rang several times with no answer. The voice mail picked up, and without thinking, I left a hurried message. "I hope you are okay. I'm still praying for you. I think maybe you've decided to parent the baby, and I understand. I know you will be a good mom." I hung up the phone and dropped the little shoes into my lap. With my face in my hands, I sobbed.

I waited exactly a month after the baby's due date, just in case, and then I packed up her room and donated all the little-girl things. I knew we might have another little girl one day, but I couldn't bear to save things that I imagined belonged to someone else. I put the ballet slippers on the top shelf of my closet, and when my sister adopted a little girl several years later, I wrapped them up and gave them to my new niece with her baby shower gift.

I was surprised by my grief and sense of loss in the weeks and months that followed. My three closest friends were pregnant or in the beginning stages of adoption during that time. I smiled as their babies were born and brought gifts and casseroles, but inside, I felt the weight of something missing in our own home. I found it hard to describe to others, so I just didn't talk about it.

The adoption agency contacted us and asked if we would like to put our profile out again for other birth moms to view. Mike and I talked about it off and on but found the subject unapproachable. It seemed that we were all hurting. A neighbor unexpectedly offered to babysit, and we went to our favorite restaurant. "We need to make a decision," I offered.

"I know. What do you want to do?" he replied.

I searched the depths of my heart and mind and spoke the truth. "I don't want to do it again." I breathed a sigh of relief.

"Me neither," he said. "It just doesn't feel right this time."

The decision felt right. We talked throughout dinner about our family and our purpose. We knew that there were other children without homes and other families who just needed a little support and a chance at reunification. We weighed the possibilities of closing our adoption profile and keeping our foster license open. We knew the hurt and uncertainty of the foster-care system. We knew it was risky to open our doors to families in need, but we just couldn't deny the peace we felt making the decision. Before we paid the bill and returned home that night, we had decided that for one year, we would keep our foster license active, and we would commit to keeping our doors wide open.

Part 2

THE FULLNESS
OF SUMMER

3

A ROCKY START

The summer we decided to open our doors again was brutal. Humidity was high, and the heat pressed in on us like a weight. The air conditioner broke on the hottest day, so we opened every window and door. Despite the heat, we didn't fail to see the humor in our situation. I propped the front door open with a brick while Mike slid the backdoor screen into place. We placed a fan in the hallway, trying to give some movement to the sticky air.

"Well, we did say we would keep the doors open. I just didn't think we were going to literally have to live like this," I said to Mike, and he laughed. It took a week to get the air-conditioning fixed, and by the time the repairman arrived, we had taken up residence in our basement like cave dwellers, hiding from the sun. The cool air began to blow just as Christine and Grace came down with the stomach flu. Christine had only been sick a handful of times in her nine years of life, and she took the illness as a personal insult. Grace, who was eight, just grabbed a bucket and a blanket and resigned herself to the bathroom floor, which was finally blessedly cool.

I slipped my bare feet between the sheets just as I heard Aaron, who was seven, crying. Pulling my covers back, I padded down the hallway and entered his room. I stroked his forehead, rinsed out the vomit bucket, and returned it to his bedside. He was the third one down with the stomach flu in a week, and I was beginning to feel exhausted. I sat down next to him on the bed and patted his back until he fell into a restless sleep. My own eyes closed, and I slept next to him just as I had when he was a baby.

I woke the next morning to the sound of Christine and Grace's happy laughter and the sun peeking through the side of the darkening shade. I could tell the girls were watching cartoons, and I could hear the soft clinking of cereal bowls and the sound of Mike's voice. Remembering it was his day off work, I smiled to myself with relief. My hand was still draped across Aaron. He was warm but not feverish and thankfully still asleep. I tucked his sheets around him, grabbed an extra blanket from his laundry basket, covered my feet, and fell back to sleep.

I woke up about an hour later with determination. Climbing silently past Aaron, I set about the task of disinfecting the entire house. I had just completed the bathroom and was carefully scrubbing the doorknobs when I heard Mike on the stairs behind me. "Looking good! The house isn't looking bad either." He chuckled at his own joke.

I turned around, looking as haggard as I felt. "Thanks. I know I look hot."

We both laughed, and then I thanked him for letting me sleep in. The past few days had been a disaster, and it felt good to have had some uninterrupted sleep. Mike returned to Christine and Grace, and I continued cleaning. I worked quietly, hoping the worst had passed. I was deep in thought when I was jolted back to reality by the ringing telephone. The caseworker on the other end of the call sounded desperate. She asked me if I could take a five-week-old that afternoon and his eighteen-month-old sister later in the week. She explained something about a hospital stay for the older child, but my mind had already wandered to the logistics of having two more children in the house. I looked around at the freshly cleaned second floor and figured I could have everything ready to go by the afternoon. I said yes.

I hung up the phone and marched downstairs to tell everyone that we had a tiny guest coming that afternoon. The girls were pleased. Grace was very good with babies and immediately went to the kitchen to start washing bottles and to locate pacifiers and receiving blankets. Christine helped clean up the breakfast dishes. Mike and I made eye contact and both let out a sigh. We were really doing this again. The fear and excitement passed between us without words. Being a foster family is a tangible way to help others, but it is often a frightening roller coaster of emotions as well, and we were jumping back in with both feet, this time knowing full well what we were getting into.

At 1:00 p.m., there was a knock at the door. By then, Aaron was awake, bathed, and feeling much better. "Nothing can keep that kid down," I thought with a laugh. He ran to the door and flung it open before I could round the corner. The caseworker stepped inside, holding a small bundle in her arms. She handed the baby to me and set his medical passport on the table by the door. It contained his name, his medical records, his Medicaid number, and little else.

The caseworker explained that his older sister was hospitalized with failure to thrive. In a hushed tone, she detailed how the little girl was losing weight rapidly, and it seemed that the mom and dad weren't feeding her regularly; they didn't seem to even understand the importance of balanced meals. The developmental pediatrician was the one who had filed the report. She felt sure that with proper encouragement, the child would begin to eat properly and regain the weight she had lost.

The caseworker knew little else, so I shook her hand and took the small diaper bag containing the clothes the baby boy's mom and dad had packed. That was more than most arrived with, and I was grateful for it. I closed the door, and a wave of sadness rushed over me. That and something else—nausea. Oh no—I was determined not to be the next in line for the stomach bug.

I set the baby on my daughter's lap. "His name is…" I didn't have time to say "Jonathan" as I ran to the bathroom.

Mike had to return to work the next day—his job at the church did not leave much time for family illness or new babies—and to my dismay, I didn't bounce back as quickly as Aaron. I spent the following day crawling back and forth between our new foster son and my bed. But our three children were still excited about the new baby and completely took on adult responsibilities the entire day. I called Grace into my room around noon and asked her if she remembered how to make the baby a bottle. She nodded proudly and recited the instructions: "Two ounces for every one scoop!" I gave her a wink and handed her Jonathan's bottle. It was hard to believe she was only in second grade. She brought the bottle back to me, and I fed the baby. I felt much better by late afternoon, and Jonathan was finally asleep.

Grace and Christine had more than earned an hour of television, so I turned on an episode of *Hannah Montana*. The theme music was enough to make my headache return, so I squeezed Aaron's hand and asked him to come upstairs with me. I ran a bath for him and began disinfecting everything once again. Aaron had rarely been able to keep still since the day he was born—often I felt exhausted before I even got out of bed just thinking about his little body in continual motion. However, bath time was one thing that could usually do the trick.

I ran the water extra warm and reached below the bathroom cabinet for the one-dollar bottle of shaving cream. Aaron squealed with delight and had his clothes off in one swift movement. I began to laugh, which took the last bit of energy out of my body. I slid to the floor and placed my hands on the cool tile.

"I'm sorry you don't feel good, Mommy." Aaron's sweet voice nearly brought me to tears. I sat that way for nearly an hour, adding hot water as needed to the tub, and listened to Aaron's seven-year-old reasoning on life. He was going to have 20 children but only one really nice, really pretty wife. He was going to be a police officer and a chef. I silently thanked God for the blessing of a son who could entertain himself. Then Jonathan began to cry. I handed Aaron a towel as I pulled the drain on the tub. He reluctantly removed himself and scowled toward the baby. I patted his body and helped him put lotion on before I attended to the baby. Finally, Jonathan's voice had reached a piercing level, and I gave Aaron a quick squeeze and turned toward the bassinet.

Aaron went to his room to get dressed as I bounced the baby on one hip and filled the bottle with my other hand. He calmed without much prompting, to my great relief. My head was beginning to pound, and the energy I had just expended proved to be too much. I put the bottle in Jonathan's mouth and plopped into the rocking chair. He was a good eater, and I wondered for a moment about the sister waiting in the hospital. "What's the story, little man?" I whispered. His eyes popped open, and for a moment, I thought he was going to answer. I smiled and then lay my head back and closed my eyes. I wanted to pray for this sweet baby, but I didn't have the energy.

I whispered, "Lord…" just as I heard a steady pounding from the room next to mine. My head had begun to hurt so much that I didn't want to call out for my son, but I did. "Aaron? Are you okay?" No answer. I called again and then resigned my exhausted body to the truth that I was going to have to go see. The pounding got louder and louder. I rounded the corner to see Aaron banging his head against the wall. A small dent in the drywall caught my attention. "Oh, no! Aaron, stop. You are going to hurt yourself."

He glanced in my direction. "That stupid baby is making me mad." I was confused—Jonathan hadn't been in our care for 24 hours. I tried compassion first. "Tell me what's bothering you," I soothed.

"Stupid baby," he responded.

"I'm not going to allow you to call him stupid. I love you very much, but I can't help you when you do this." My head felt on fire, and I resisted the urge to sink to the floor again. I decided to stay quiet and prevent myself from passing out. Bracing myself against the doorframe, I continued to feed Jonathan. Aaron persisted but with the commitment of someone who had recently recovered from the stomach flu. He hit his head one more time and then yelled, "The *stu*—I mean, the *dumb* baby doesn't even have a name!"

Despite myself, I started to laugh. Aaron did too. "What do you mean, he doesn't have a name?" I questioned. Then I realized I had been so sick, I hadn't even told anyone the little guy's name. "His name is Jonathan, and he's five weeks old. He just needs a place to stay for a little while. I know you aren't feeling good. I don't feel good either. I'm sorry I didn't tell you more about him. I know you are so good with babies. I'm sure you are going to be a fantastic helper once you feel better. Would you like to snuggle with me in my bed when I get Jonathan back to sleep, and we can look at some books?"

Aaron hit the wall with his fist one more time, but there was no emotion connected to it. He told me no even as he began to survey the bookshelf for his favorite stories.

"I'm going to put Jonathan to bed, and you can come in when-ever you're ready, okay?" I said the words calmly, but I just wanted to cry. Thankfully, Jonathan fell immediately back to sleep, and just as my head hit the pillow, I felt Aaron sink into the pillow next to me and watched him close his eyes.

As I laid there, willing my body to heal, I reflected on the first day of our one-year commitment. Following God's plan for our family had gotten off to a rocky start, and I hadn't anticipated it. I foolishly thought that if we chose to keep our doors open for a year, the road would rise to meet us. I pictured the sun shining each morning and a house full of laughter and good times. I knew that fostering was a tough job. We had already been fostering for six years and knew to expect the challenges, but I had envisioned things to be different this time. We had committed to the Lord, for crying out loud—surely He would provide a stomach-flu-free home. Even as I lay there thinking those thoughts, I felt the hand of my heavenly Father on me. I placed one of my own hands on my now-sleeping son and the other on my new baby foster son and fell asleep.

4

ILL PREPARED

On the last day of June, the caseworker called. Juniper, Jonathan's big sister, was cleared to be released that evening. I arranged for a neighbor to watch the other kids until Mike finished work. I had recently become obsessed with making freezer meals and pulled a veggie lasagna from the freezer and popped it into the oven, setting the timer and patting myself on the back all at the same time. I felt like I could do anything. "Keeping our doors open won't change a thing," I thought. I was a superstar mom, and I knew it. I looked around and wished someone were there to validate me.

Just then Aaron popped his head over the counter and made a gagging face. "Veggie lasagna? Why, Mom? Why?" He fell to the floor writhing in an exaggerated death scene.

"I hope you have a career as an actor someday." I reached down and pulled him up by his one extended arm. He opened one eye and sighed.

My bubble was only deflated for a moment. I was about to meet Jonathan's older sister. She was 18 months old, and I was so excited about all the preschool things we were going to do. I made a mental list as I slipped on my shoes and said goodbye to the kids. We could go to the Children's Museum, the water park, story time at

41

the library…I would have to pick up some pretty sundresses too! My daughters were eight and nine at the time and had grown tired of playing dress-up with Mama.

On the drive to the hospital, I reminded myself that this little girl was also hurting and scared. She had just lost her own mama. I didn't yet know the story, but I knew at the very least that this little girl would need some tender loving care as she adjusted to our family. I promised myself that I would take things slow, and hopefully, Juniper would return home stronger and healthier.

My hastily written instructions were jammed into the back pocket of my linen shorts. The weather was still sweltering hot, but I wanted to look a little nice while meeting the hospital staff and my new charge as well. The drive to the city took about an hour, and by the time I reached the hospital, I kicked myself for driving the 12-passenger van. I knew it wouldn't fit into any of the parking garages at the children's hospital. I watched the clock tick steadily forward as I tried to find a space large enough. Finally, I eased into a space and dug as much change as I could find from the ashtray to feed the meter.

Scanning the landscape, I located the hospital about three blocks away. I began to walk while reading over my notes from the caseworker. Juniper, 18 months, Children's Hospital, fourth floor. I began to sweat and looked at my watch to check the time again. I had ten minutes to make it by the appointed time. I started to jog.

The hospital doors swished open, and a blast of cool air hit my skin. I had made it. I asked the lady at the help desk how to get to the fourth floor. She looked up at me and jumped a little before recovering. "Oh!" She quickly smiled and gave me directions. "Just take the first hallway right and then turn left at the third hallway. You will look for the blue elevator on the right. At the third floor, you will exit the elevator and go to your right. You will see a desk there—pass that desk and go to your left, and take the green elevator on the left to the fourth floor. That is a locked unit, so you will have to show ID when you get there. Do you have your ID?" Thankfully I did.

I smiled and tried to repeat her directions again in my head. "I'm Superwoman," I reminded myself. "I've got this." But I did not have this. I wandered for the next few minutes until an elderly woman noticed my confusion.

"Where are you trying to go?" she asked warmly.

"Fourth floor," I answered with a sigh.

"I'll take you there," she replied, and I followed.

We entered the blue elevator, and I caught a glimpse of myself in the silver doors. "Oh no!" I exclaimed as I quickly began to smooth my hair and dab at my sweating forehead. "No wonder people were staring at me."

The woman laughed softly. "Oh dear, you look just fine." She paused for a moment. "It's hot out there today. I'll show you where the ladies' room is on our way, and you can freshen up a bit."

I ducked into the woman's room and splashed water on my face. The woman walked me the rest of the way to the fourth floor and wished me a good day. I was truly grateful for her kindness and told her so as I stepped up to the desk in front of the locked entrance to the fourth floor.

I handed the stern-looking woman my identification, and she peered over the top of her glasses at me. "I don't have you on the list. Who are you here for?"

I smiled and said confidently, "Juniper Jones." The woman ran her finger slowly down her computer screen, and I shifted my weight to stretch my now-tender calf muscles. "Maybe I should take up running again," I thought to myself. That three-block jog had about done me in.

The woman shook her head. "You aren't on this list."

I caught myself before letting out a frustrated sigh. "I'm her new foster mom."

"Hmm…" She drew out the sound for an uncomfortably long time and picked up the phone. "I have a girl here who says she's the foster mom of a patient." I winced as she said the word "girl" and "foster" with what felt like a stab. She listened for a moment and hung up. She eyed me again and stood without a word. She walked to the door and waved her badge in front of the lock pad. "Room 442, end of the hall to the left." Then she walked away. I wasn't sure how, but I had really hit a nerve with her. I tried to shake off the sinking feeling. I was not feeling super anymore.

I sucked in a breath and walked toward room 442. A nurse noticed me, smiled, and offered to help me find the way. She sounded relieved that I was there to get Juniper. "I'm glad you're here—June-Bug is ready to get out of here!" As we rounded the corner, I spotted the back of a high chair just outside of the room. The chair was facing away from me, but Juniper's little arms were reaching behind her at an impossibly odd angle. Her blonde hair curled wildly above the back of the seat. Just then, she peeked her head around the chair and squealed sharply. Her eyes were the lightest shade of blue I had ever seen.

A woman stepped out of the room just then and shook her head. "What a mess! Oh, good, you must be the foster mom—we've been waiting for you. We tried to fix her hair but…"

I turned to the little girl and saw the remains of a pink ribbon mangled and plastered to her cheek. The nurse unbuckled Juniper from her high chair and began to give me instructions. "We have all her NG tube supplies right here—you'll need to feed her every two hours. She pulls the tube out between feedings, so I'm sorry to say you'll have to place it each time."

I put my hand up to stop her. "What's an NG tube?" The two

women glanced at one another, and I saw worry pass between them. "A nasogastric tube is a feeding tube." She spoke slowly and with a measure of disbelief. "We were told she would be going to a medical therapeutic foster home."

I shook my head. "Just a regular foster mom here."

One of the nurses sat on the edge of the couch, placing Juniper on her lap. "Well, I guess we have some teaching to do. Come on, it isn't that hard."

Juniper's body never stopped moving, so the first step in feeding her was getting her to be still. The nurse showed me how to swaddle her using a large blanket. Just like a baby—a really big, really strong baby. I practiced till Juniper was red-faced and furious. I folded the blanket into a triangle, placing her feet at the narrow part. Folding one of her arms next to her side, I wrapped the blanket tightly over her shoulder and tucked it against her opposite leg. I folded the bottom up while placing my hand firmly on her free arm. Then I completed the task with the other arm. Her body relaxed. "Snug as a June-Bug in a rug," I whispered.

The nurses were surprised. "That was the hardest part. Now for the feeding tube…" one of them encouraged. I didn't want to admit that I was terrified. They showed me how to measure the tube from nostril to ear to chest. I kept my arms around Juniper as I watched the nurse feed the tube into Juniper's nostril. The room began to tilt, and I felt like I was going to vomit. I cursed myself for my weak stomach and forced my eyes back onto the project at hand. The tube was properly placed, and I put the stethoscope into my ears and listened to her chest as the nurse showed me how to safely check the placement. Once everything was placed properly, the PediaSure drip began. It took a long time to feed her, and she began to become antsy again. I sang to her, forgetting how embarrassed I was about singing in front of others. We practiced three more times before the nurses declared that I was trained. I didn't feel qualified, but I didn't argue.

I could tell Juniper was glad to be done with my clumsy excuse for medical attention. As I unwrapped her, she jumped from the bed and moved across the room like a Tasmanian devil. She was a wonder to watch, and I began to realize why the staff were so determined to see her into her new home that night. She climbed the back of the couch, bent a window blind, and twirled her body in her bedsheets all in one movement. I could barely keep my eyes on her, much less my hands. She found a toy beneath the bed and put it into her mouth. I saw my opportunity and scooped her up.

One of the nurses quickly gathered her things and shoved them into a plastic drawstring bag. "We'll walk you to your car—we have to do a car seat inspection." My hand flew to my forehead; I had completely forgotten the car, which was parked three blocks away. I explained the situation, and the nurses agreed to stay with Juniper in the lobby while I retrieved the van.

I jogged the three blocks to the van as the sun disappeared. I couldn't believe it had become so late. I rounded the block and saw a man leaning against a telephone pole just next to the parking meter. I felt my stomach turn as I glanced around to see if there were any other people around. A man and a woman were walking just behind me, and I decided to just continue to move with confidence. I really didn't have time to be overly cautious. Juniper was waiting back in the hospital lobby with two harried nurses. I whispered a prayer: "Lord, please walk with me."

I noticed a paper fluttering as I approached the car and plucked it from the windshield. I slid into the driver's seat and locked the doors in one swift movement. The man and woman passed the van just as I clicked the lock. The man outside the door made no move to acknowledge me. I glanced at the paper long enough to realize what it was. Shoving the parking ticket into the center console, I made my way back to the hospital.

Tube feedings were a breeze compared to buckling Juniper into the car seat. She didn't make a fuss, but her body moved like a spaghetti noodle. Her leg was pressed next to her ear as I wrangled one limb into the restraint. As soon as I had all points buckled, I realized she had maneuvered her head out of the shoulder strap. Perplexed, I climbed back into her seat and reworked the buckle until there was barely room to place two fingers between the straps. I returned to my seat and smiled in the rearview mirror at her. "It's okay, June-Bug." Her clear blue eyes met mine, and she let out a low growl. "Okay, I'm okay with that," I told her calmly.

I talked to her on the ride home and tried to keep my voice calm and reassuring. "I know you don't know me, and I'm sorry this is so scary. Jonathan is staying with me too. You will be safe. I promise we will get this all worked out soon, little one." She didn't make eye contact again, but she did stop growling. Once she was quiet, I made a quick call to Mike to let him know I was finally on my way.

We pulled into the driveway about three hours after I'd planned to be home. Mike had the kids tucked into bed and was washing the dinner dishes when I stepped through the door. He turned to look at me. "What happened to you?" he said with amusement. I was sweaty, dirty, frazzled, and looking a bit defeated. I had three hospital bags draped over one arm and a sleeping toddler in the other.

"I don't even know where to start," I answered. I wasn't sure I had the strength to recount the entire adventure. I looked at the clock and realized it was time for another feeding. "You are never going to believe this!" I exclaimed as I carefully unpacked the medical supplies.

5

GAINING CLARITY

Before I go any further, I think this is a good place to stop and address my imagination. Of course, by "imagination," I mean "tendency to be delusional." I have always had a lively ability to envision myself in various scenarios. I love a good daydream more than just about anything. Even as I write this book, I must resist the urge to change my name to something great like Cleopatra or Mirabella or Amiya. As soon as my baby sister, Rebecca, was born, I became convinced that names ending with a soft "a" sound had the magic ability to change an average person into someone delicate and beautiful. I was certain as a preschooler that my sister's name only added to her striking beauty.

I'm easily distracted by my tendency toward daydream. I say to myself, "Kristin, you must write one more chapter, and then you can reward yourself by staring out the window with wandering thoughts." In my daydreams, I admit, I almost always play the quiet hero. I'm usually very beautiful, with flowing brunette hair that curls ever so slightly at the ends. My freckles are a cute sprinkling just across my nose, and my smooth, flawless skin is radiant. I am always smiling and speaking in a wonderfully soft voice. I am wearing the cutest casual trendy clothes. I imagine that others might even call my style "effortless." In my imagination, I take all of life's trials in stride, and I stand confidently in the face of adversity.

I return to these conjured-up notions of myself often. When I picture myself as a mother, I feel chubby little baby arms wrapped around my shoulders. I hear the sweet giggles of toddlers, and I welcome teenagers into my home without trepidation. Nothing shocks me, and I handle all parenting hurdles with an air of grace. In my daydream, I see the faces of appreciative birth parents and caseworkers. They regard me as an ally, and they know that I desire to play this small, selfless role in helping reunite a family.

Don't put the book down! Please, stay with me. You have to know my fantasy in order to feel my reality.

The reality is more like this: I have very straight dark-blonde hair that is neither flowing nor beautiful. My fashion sense could be called "thrift-store chic," only drop the "chic" and add "I got this on 99 Cent Sunday at Goodwill." My voice is loud, and my patience is thin. I love people fiercely, and sometimes my passion gets me into confrontations with people whom I have deemed bullies. I fight for justice and equality, especially when confronting an adult who embarrassed my little sister when we were in high school or refusing to spend one more penny at a local bagel shop until a staff member apologizes to my brother for talking to him in a condescending tone. I am quick to defend those I love and slow to apologize when I am wrong. I overthink things and feel emotions to my core. Many nights, I give my anxieties to the Lord, only to pick them up around 2:00 a.m., deciding that I am a stronger bearer of the world's burdens than my heavenly Father Himself!

My daydream is still lovely, and I enjoy visiting it sometimes, but I must let it go to tell this story well. I've been humbled by recognizing my imperfection. In my weakness, I have learned to lean on the strength of others. Somewhere between my fantasy and my reality, there is the real me, cracked open and on display. Open to correction, open to new ideas, open to others, open to love and be loved.

Thank you for sticking with me on this diversion. Honesty is the first step to clarity of perspective. Imagine yourself in the driver's seat of a car. You are traveling a road well known to you. You are going someplace you've been often—maybe your child's school or the home of a close friend. You're singing along to the radio and lost in thought about all you have to do later that day. There are clouds overhead but no rain in the forecast. The sky begins to sprinkle, but you pay no attention. You continue driving with full confidence. The rain falls softly on your windshield, the music floats from your speakers, and you continue driving, nearly unaware of the storm brewing and unconcerned about your increasingly obstructed visibility as each drop of rain blurs the road in front of you. A few more miles pass, and reflexively, you turn the wipers on. That first stroke leaves your window cloudy, and for a moment you are snapped into the present. You flick the headlights on, and as the wipers sweep across your window a second time, the world around you becomes crystal clear. You suddenly see with great clarity everything you had been missing before.

Life can be like that. We often think we know where we are going. The road before us seems familiar and our perspective clear…and then life sends a sprinkle, reminding us that our perspective has been cloudy all along. When I began my year of openness, I believed I knew the road that lay before me. When the cloud around my vision began to lift, I began to grasp the world of perspectives I had never known existed.

6

RIGHTEOUS ANGER

June and Jonathan's developmental pediatrician expressed concern about both children's growth. She was their doctor before they came to our home, and we kept going to her for continuity. She wanted carefully documented charts of everything the children ate or drank as well as weekly weight checks at her office, which was a 45-minute drive from our house. The doctor spoke to me in a tone that implied I was stupid. She spoke slowly and without emotion. When I tried to ask a question, she sighed. I began to feel like I was on trial each week, and soon, my nerves were shot.

One day while I was in the office, she let it slip that she was the one who had filed the report against the children's parents. She had filed multiple reports against them over June's short life. I felt angry toward their parents as I thought about the children being neglected and the parents' refusal to learn to feed them properly.

Even as I felt the burst of righteous indignation, I felt another complex feeling. It sat in the pit of my stomach as I was listening to the pediatrician speak slowly to me about the correct way to administer June's medication. I fought the urge to lash out at her and instead pushed down the nagging feeling that the doctor might be the one who had created this problem with the parents. If she talked to me this way, how had she been talking to them? Had she even tried to assist them, or had she just barreled forward, believing herself to be the best judge? Was something more going on with the children than a simple case of neglect? A knot began to form in my stomach. I found myself terrified of being reported myself.

One night before an appointment, June began vomiting. She continued throughout the night. I couldn't get her to keep one feeding down. By the third bath and fresh set of jammies, I began to worry about dehydration. I sat with June on my lap and called the nurse's line for my other children's pediatrician. The nurse on call gave me steps to take to make sure she stayed hydrated. She told me to check her diapers and make sure they were still wet. I did, and I felt relieved. By 4:00 a.m., I realized she was also running a fever. She was exhausted, and so was I. I grabbed a few blankets from the foot of my bed and laid them on the floor of the bathroom. I sat down beside her and stroked her curly hair. Her body, which was normally in constant motion, had never been this still. It was frightening and fascinating at the same time.

I took her temperature under her tiny arm, careful not to wake her. The thermometer beeped at 100.1. I pulled it quickly away from her, kicking myself for not remembering that it made a sound signaling that it was finished. But she didn't move. I slipped the thermometer onto the counter and lay my head next to hers on her tiny pallet. Resting my arm over her, I began to drift off.

I jolted awake around five as I remembered the rules for the doctor's office and realized I couldn't take her to the children's hospital for her weight check. The hospital had signs posted everywhere asking patients not to come to appointments if they'd had a fever or cough within the last 24 hours, since some of the patients suffered from compromised immune systems. I knew I had to cancel the appointment. My hand was shaking as I dialed the number and left the message for the office. I explained what was happening and why I would be keeping the children home. I wondered to myself why my heart was racing. As I tended to June the rest of that long night, I realized I was afraid of the doctor. I was afraid of her criticism and her power.

It turned out that I was right to worry. June recovered from the illness quickly, as most toddlers do. By ten o'clock the following day, she was fever-free and ready to go. I was groggy from the long night and found that it took extra effort to keep up with her as she tried to climb the kitchen counters, bookshelves, and basement stairs. She toppled a stack of clean laundry baskets as I fixed a bottle for Jonathan. Around four in the afternoon, as our older kids were about to get off the bus from school, I sat in the family room finishing up a bottle with Jonathan. Juniper was bouncing in her jumper swing, which was attached to the doorframe. My eyes felt heavy, and holding the lids open had begun to feel like a feat of superhuman strength. I shuffled to the kitchen and placed the empty bottle in the sink. Jonathan burped quickly. Relieved, I placed him in the portable crib just as the phone rang. It was the Department of Child Services. I answered just before it went to voice mail. "Hello," I said as cheerfully as possible.

"Hello, this is Ms. Hopkins. I am the caseworker for…" She paused, and I heard the rustling of papers. "Juniper and Jonathan," she continued, her voice flat. "Why did you miss Juniper's appointment today?"

"I…um…" I stuttered. "She was sick—wait, how do you know about the appointment?"

"A report was filed today stating that you were a no-show to Juniper's appointment. The doctor is concerned that you do not take her health seriously. She feels that you don't understand the importance of this child's health and well-being. It is very important that you take her to all of her appointments and arrive promptly."

I reached up and pushed my glasses onto my forehead to rub my aching eyes as I thought of how to respond. With my voice as calm as possible, I replied, "Juniper was running a fever. I left a message at the doctor's office at five a.m. letting them know that I would not be bringing her in today per the office policy."

"Oh, I see. Well, it is really important that you keep all appointments."

"I will not expose other children to illness."

"You don't have to get short with me! I really don't like your tone right now."

"I really don't like being reprimanded for following the office policy."

"This is a warning, Mrs. Berry. I will not tolerate this type of carelessness."

I sucked in a breath before responding again. "I am not careless with my children, Ms. Hopkins. Please don't imply that I am. I will call the doctor's office and get this sorted out right now."

Just then, I noticed Juniper had wiggled free from her jumper and was scooting toward the dog door. Half her body was through the opening, and I could hear the bus rounding the corner as well. "I really have to go. I'll get this worked out. Thank you for the call." I hung up the phone before she could answer. I knew I might hear about it later, but Juniper was now completely out of the dog door. I set the phone down and ran into the backyard after June.

I caught her as she began to climb the play set. "No, June, you can't go outside without an adult. Besides, the big kids are here. Come on, let's go get them!" I started toward the house as the doorbell began to ring and ring and ring. Jogging toward the door with the toddler in one arm, I reached it by the sixth ring.

"That's enough," I said to the three children standing on the front step. Christine stood with one hand on her hip and the other one raised as if to begin a lecture.

"Not now, Christine," I snapped. Ushering them inside, I got the little kids settled and then made the big kids a snack. "I need to make a phone call. Will you guys be okay watching a cartoon for a little bit?" They all shouted yes with excitement.

I scooped June up and plopped her into her crib before shutting myself in my room to make the phone call. I could hear her fussing from behind my closed door but knew something needed to be done about this doctor. I called the doctor's office first and explained to the pleasant lady at the front desk what had happened. I allowed myself to be firm but not angry. She put me through to the doctor's voice mail.

I then called a friend who worked at the same location to find out how to file a grievance. Within the next half hour, I called the doctor's supervisor—the supervisor of pediatrics—and also wrote a formal complaint to the board. In my letter, I explained the reason for our canceled appointment. I copied word for word the hospital policy on not coming in if a child has had a fever within the previous 24 hours. I then explained the repercussions for a foster family when they have a report filed. Not only was the report false, stating that the appointment was a no-show and implying negligence on my part, but it could have been avoided with a simple call to check on the details of the cancellation.

When I was a child, my parents taught me to face confrontation with a calm and factual approach. They also taught me to give others the benefit of the doubt. The latter was hard to do in this situation, but I promised myself that as a reward for keeping my cool, I would have to plan a girls' night with my friends soon to vent how I really felt about the situation.

As I closed my computer, I thought about the skills necessary to defend oneself in situations like these. I was still upset about the accusation against my family, but I felt confident that I would be able to advocate for myself if this went further. I scooped Juniper out of her crib, where she had been entertaining herself with a pile of toys. She wrapped her little arms around me and squeezed. It wasn't exactly a hug, but it made me smile. "Sorry I had to leave you for a bit, June-Bug." She wiggled against my embrace, and I took a good look at her as she ran on tiny legs into the family room to join the older children. I glanced at the clock and cursed myself for letting it get so late. I began sterilizing June's equipment and wondered again what had truly happened with her mom and dad. Caring for these two children had turned out to be a lot more than I had bargained for. Was this really a case of neglect, or were these children caught in a system fraught with ill-equipped professionals and layered with misunderstanding?

June and Jonathan each had to eat every two hours. The children never ate at the same time, which meant hourly feedings. Jonathan ate with no interest and took nearly an hour to take each bottle. By the time Jonathan finished, it was time to prepare June's tube feeding. Mike and I were blurry eyed and cranky after the first week. By the second week, I was jumpy and on edge. By week six, I was beginning to feel truly depressed. I was isolated from the rest of the world and couldn't remember the last time I had carried on an adult conversation.

One morning after Mike had gone to work and the older children were placed safely on the bus, I took Jonathan in my arms and sunk to the floor in despair. I knew if I didn't feed him soon, his feeding would bump into Juniper's and the whole day would be off schedule. I felt defeated. I had to face the fact that I was nobody's hero.

Just as I began to cry, the phone rang. I groped around on the floor next to my bed, still balancing the newborn in one arm. I cursed myself for not putting the phone on silent and dreaded the inevitable waking of June. I answered it before the second ring, whispering as I crawled past June's crib and out the door.

"Hello…why are you whispering?" my friend chuckled.

The tears began to fall. I shut the door behind me and sobbed, "I don't know what I'm doing. This is too much, I just can't keep up. I thought I could, but I can't."

My friend's tone changed. "I'll be there in 30 minutes, okay? You don't have to do this alone."

I protested, thinking about all her responsibilities with her own children.

"If our roles were reversed, would you do this for me?" she asked.

"Of course," I answered without hesitation.

"Well then, why are you refusing my help? Are you too good for me?" she snapped back jokingly.

I laughed. "You're right."

"I know I am. See you soon," she said as she hung up the phone.

Megan came through the front door balancing two kids, Dunkin' Donuts coffee, a box of donuts, and a 42-ounce Mountain Dew. I set Jonathan down in his Pack 'n Play and ran to the door to help her.

"I've got this!" she said as she nearly toppled over, along with a toddler, the diaper bag, and the precious cup of coffee. I grabbed her littlest one and laughed too. "Okay, okay, I get it. You've made your point. I will ask for help from now on." We talked through the morning as she helped me feed the kids and get my house back in order. I told her about our commitment to help others for a year.

I told her about feeling the poetic calling to keep the doors open. Even as I said it, the words felt silly. Was I a preteen with a rose-colored view of life?

Megan paused for a minute as she let the words soak in and then responded, "Maybe keeping your door open means you will learn to accept help even as you are offering it to others." Megan was right, of course. Mike and I needed to allow others around us to take part in the narrative God was writing for our family.

The report filed by the developmental pediatrician stayed in our file along with my letter disputing the report and a Post-it note in our caseworker's handwriting that read, "Report unfounded." I felt angry every time I thought about the injustice of it. I put in a request for a change in developmental pediatrician but had to wait for approval from Medicaid, the caseworker, and the parents. While I waited for approval, I was able to get permission to do weight checks at the office of a local doctor. The doctor had seen all my children and was very familiar with our family. On the day of our first weight check, she asked questions about all the children but took extra time to care for June and Jonathan. She pointed me toward some feeding resources and put in a referral for First Steps, a program for early childhood intervention. I exited the office with June safely strapped into her stroller and Jonathan perched on my hip. Christine, Grace, and Aaron were on summer break, and they happily trailed behind us toward the car.

A few weeks later, the phone rang again. I looked at the ID and my heart sank. It was the doctor's office. Fear ran through me as I answered, and I braced myself for the fallout.

"Hello, is this Juniper's foster mom?"

"Yes."

"This is Juniper's developmental pediatrician. I'm calling because there seems to be a misunderstanding. I understand that you canceled her appointment because of vomiting and fever."

"Yes," I replied in a measured tone.

"Well, I didn't know that you canceled. I'm sorry for the misunderstanding."

"Misunderstanding?" I responded, my voice growing stronger. "You reported me to the Department of Child Services. Do you do that to all your patients? Did you make any attempt to gather the details on our absence, or did you just jump to conclusions?"

"I don't appreciate your tone, Mrs. Smith."

"Smith is not my last name—you don't even know my last name. You put my family at risk. I now have to work to remove that report from my file. Your report could have caused me to lose my license. You caused heartache and fear in my family. You could have avoided this with a simple phone call to me or even a call to your own office administrator to get the recorded message I left concerning your policy on seeing children who have had a fever within the last 24 hours."

"I was just doing my job, ma'am."

"Please continue to report suspected abuse and neglect, but please do so responsibly. I accept your apology. If we do need to work together in the future, I hope we can do so professionally. Goodbye."

"Goodbye."

It wasn't exactly an apology, but I still felt vindicated. My hands were shaking as I clicked the phone off. I wondered again how families were supposed to navigate a system where lack of communication and care for others seemed to be the norm. Over the years, our family would face false reports, misunderstandings, and investigations numerous times. We learned to document every bump, bruise, and paper cut.

We also learned that there really are children in danger in biological families as well as foster families. Those sworn to protect children were often dealing with limited information and had to rely on gut instinct.

7

OPENING THE DOOR
A LITTLE WIDER

Our days began to feel more manageable as June and Jonathan settled into their feeding schedule. Visiting our local pediatrician for weight checks instead of driving an hour to the city each week opened up an extra three or four hours a week in our family schedule. I began to feel like we had our life back.

One summer morning after our weight check, I buckled everyone in and headed to the donut shop for a treat. I was surprised at the lightness in my own step. Meeting with a professional who encouraged rather than criticized had changed my entire attitude. I felt that I could face anything. At the donut shop, even June got in on the action. She still refused to eat most meals, but her fascination with food had grown. She smashed her donut into a sticky mess and then licked her fingers tentatively. I glanced in the rearview mirror to see her put her tiny index finger between her lips and stick her tongue out just far enough for a taste.

Aaron's car seat was jammed next to hers. They were so close that Juniper could reach into his seat. And she did. "No, June-Bug!" Aaron exclaimed as she wiped a sticky hand onto his knee. I could hear the tone in his voice rising and feel the familiar tension before the meltdown.

"Aaron, it's okay. Mama has wipes. Can you wait just one minute, please? I will get you a wipe." I talked soft and low, willing Aaron to calm down so the day wouldn't be ruined. I could see our favorite park just ahead and slowed the car. "Aaron, I'm pulling into the park now. I have wipes, and we can even have some time to play!" I tried to use my most enthusiastic tone. He wasn't buying it. Parking the car in the shade of a tree, I noted that we were the only people at the park. Thankful for that little bit of luck, I suggested Christine and Grace head out to the playground. "I'll watch from the car." I felt a pang of guilt as Christine glanced back at me with a hard expression.

I had a clear view of the playground, and the day was pleasantly warm with a nice breeze. I opened all the windows and the double side doors as well. I turned to Aaron and began wiping the sticky parts. His face was rigid and angry, and his eyes were blank. When he was clean, I unbuckled him and set him on my lap. June was still happily licking her fingers, and Jonathan was sound asleep. Aaron's body was unmoving. I took each little arm and wrapped it around me. Then I placed my arms around his body and squeezed with firm pressure. His body began to relax, and I breathed my own sigh of relief. Aaron loved having babies around, but he still longed to be the baby. He wasn't one to sit still, so I enjoyed the moment of stillness with my son. He didn't usually calm so easily, which led me to wonder if my own sense of calm had rubbed off on him.

Aaron joined the girls at the playground, and I set about the task of cleaning Juniper. I first cleaned her entire body with a wet wipe and then unbuckled her to assess the damage to the car seat. She was happy to be free and climbed over and under the van seats while I wiped her car seat and threw pieces of donut in the trash.

After I finished, I began to unbuckle Jonathan to take the children to the playground.

June bolted. Her tiny body was down the steps of the van and racing full speed toward the playground before I could shout, "Wait!" I called to the girls to catch her while struggling with the straps to Jonathan's seat. When he was finally free, I caught up to the girls, who had captured June halfway to the nearest road. My heart was pounding at the thought of what could have happened. I set the baby carrier down next to the girls and scooped June into my arms. I kissed my daughters on the tops of their heads and asked them to sit with the baby. They agreed, and I marched June back to the van, where I had been keeping the most dreaded of all baby gear—the leash.

Hers was disguised as a backpack with the face of a monkey, attached to a long tail with a handle. I had avoided using it because I was afraid of what others would think. "Too bad, little girl," I told her as I strapped her into what would eventually be known as her "backpack." She wiggled, trying to get free, but complied. We spent the rest of our time at the park that way—me holding the tail and June trying to see just how far she could go.

Grace took an interest in June's and Jonathan's feeding schedules. She watched intently as I placed the NG tube for each of June's feedings. She learned to listen to June's chest to make sure the tube was placed properly. She helped pour PediaSure carefully into the tube, and she waited as the formula dripped slowly. Grace showed more patience than the rest of us combined. She entertained June during the long hours spent feeding and carefully laid NG supplies on the counter to air-dry after.

Grace also delighted in holding Jonathan while he lazily took his bottle. She would prop him on one arm with the bottle resting on her chin and then use her other hand to hold a book, turning the pages with her thumb. I watched in awe and thought about our commitment to help others and accept help. My little daughter was proving to be a part of the support system that strengthened June-Bug, Jonathan, and the entire family.

Visits with June and Jonathan's family were scheduled once a week at a visitation center in the city. Each week, I felt a sick feeling as I pulled into the weed-infested parking lot. I didn't know the parents, and I wasn't allowed to see them at visits. The procedure of pulling into the parking lot ten minutes early and then hiding away in the foster-parent waiting room did nothing to ease my uncertainty.

As I trudged up the three flights of stairs with five children, I thought about the way birth families must be feeling about the foster families. We had been placed on opposing sides without our consent when, at our core, we were fighting for the same thing. I was certain that Juniper and Jonathan's mom and dad wanted a safe place for their children to live, and that's what I wanted too. I resolved to meet the parents that day. I printed pictures for them earlier that morning, which were tucked into the diaper bag. I also had a list of new medications to help control the seizures Juniper had been suffering. I reached into the diaper bag and put both items into my back pocket.

When I reached the top floor, I smiled at the woman doing check-in and silently prayed that she would be friendly. "Hi, I'm here with Juniper and Jonathan." She gave me a half smile, and I was encouraged. "I need to pass on some medical information to Mom and Dad. I'll just chat with them really quickly when I bring the kids back." It was a tactic I had learned from my son's former foster mom. Just act like you know what you are doing and be kind. The lady at the front desk sized me up with a glance and then agreed to let me go back.

I went to the waiting room and tried to calm the butterflies in my stomach. While the assumption within the foster-care system is often that birth parents and foster families are on opposing sides, I had learned that we are all human and that often a family just needs support to become stronger and healthier. I also knew from experience that it feels better for everyone when we assume the best about others. When I was called back, I took a deep breath and then gathered the children and my things. I prayed silently that God would give me the right words to say to make a connection with this family.

Jonathan wiggled in my arms as I draped the heavy diaper bag over my shoulder. Juniper's fingers were uncharacteristically squeezing my own. It was the first time I wasn't worried about losing her. Dark-paneled hallways greeted us as I stared down at the worn green carpet. We rounded the corner into a room painted bright yellow. The color was an assault to the senses. Mom was sitting uncomfortably on an orange-and-brown couch in the corner, and Dad was waiting expectantly at the door. A supervisor sat on an old plastic chair in the opposite corner. She made a face that resembled a smile as she regarded me. I nodded to her and stuck my hand out to shake Dad's hand. Mom didn't move, but Juniper released my hand and climbed up the legs of her father before I could even say hello. I laughed despite the situation, and so did Dad.

Mom still hadn't moved from the couch or made eye contact. At first, I was offended, but then a wave of compassion came over me. I suddenly felt myself in her position. I saw myself sitting on the couch of a visitation room, only allowed to see my children once a week with a supervisor watching and judging my every move. My heart ached at the thought of my own children limited to seeing me only once a week. My observation zoomed out, and I could see the ragged furniture, the painfully bright walls, the bare light bulb, and the ancient broken toys strewn about in a room that was less than child-friendly. My heart broke, and I walked over to Mom and placed the baby in her lap. I crouched down beside her and said, "I'm Kristin. It's nice to meet you. You have a beautiful family."

I reached in my back pocket and retrieved the pictures. When I handed them to her, she looked up at me quickly and then looked away. She squeezed her baby tightly, and I took my cue to leave. I remembered the medication list and stopped quickly to go over it with Dad. He nodded and smiled before folding it and putting it in his pocket.

Over the next few weeks, Mom and Dad asked us to come in at the beginning of each visit. We only talked for a few minutes each week, but I began to look forward to seeing them. We chatted and exchanged important information as well as funny stories, usually about Juniper's adventures. During each visit, I noticed similarities between June's mannerisms and her dad's. I witnessed a smile shared by both mother and son. It warmed my heart to see them together.

I began to feel increasingly uncomfortable about why the children were removed in the first place. I knew I was only getting a glimpse of this family, but they seemed loving toward their children and genuinely hopeful that this circumstance would have a peaceful resolution. They weren't at all how I had pictured them when I was told the children were neglected. I had imagined a family too preoccupied with themselves to feed their children, but the people I saw before me were just a couple trying to get by.

One afternoon, Mike got a call from the caseworker. She told him that Dad's grandfather was in the hospital and had at most a few more days to live. The caseworker told Mike that Mom and Dad really wanted his grandpa to see the children one last time. "You don't have to bring the kids to the hospital, but maybe we could work something out. We usually don't do things like this…" She trailed off.

"No problem," Mike responded. "Of course we'll bring the kids there. What is the address? Is it okay to give Dad my number so we can arrange a time?"

The caseworker fumbled for a moment, surprised at his response. I wasn't surprised though. Mike and I had learned over the years that the parents we are working with were usually just people like us who were going through a hard time. He would do this for a friend, so of course he would do this for Juniper and Jonathan's family. He hung up the phone and explained the plan to me. It would be the first time in months that the family would be together outside of the Department of Child Services.

Mike and I left Christine, Grace, and Aaron with a sitter. We both really liked Mom and Dad, but we were unsure how this extended family reunion was going to go. It was about five o'clock when we pulled up outside of the dingy nursing home on the outskirts of the city. We each unbuckled a child and headed for the door. The woman at the front desk was crisp and measured in her tone.

"Can I help you?" she said in a voice that told me she absolutely did not want to help me.

"I'm here to see Mr. Smith," I said shakily.

"And who are you?" she responded.

I stumbled over my words. "These are his great-grandchildren." I gestured toward Mike, who had Jonathan in the car carrier and Juniper on his hip.

"Hmmm." Her response was drawn out and unamused. I felt slightly offended that she didn't at least think the kids were cute enough to prompt a smile. "Room 224. End of the hall to the left." She returned to her work without another glance. I gave her a hard look before I turned on my heel and walked toward the room. We rounded the corner and immediately heard the buzz of human activity. We realized quickly that it was coming from room 224.

In the center of the room, a small hospital bed was elevated slightly, and a large man with curly gray hair was propped on two pillows. He was dressed in his own clothes with a gray cardigan and a blanket draped over his legs. His oxygen tank was on the floor next to the bed, and an oxygen line snaked along the mattress and up to his face. He was smiling at the room around him. Every inch was filled with family members of all ages. I thought we wouldn't fit inside, but those closest to the door made way for us to squeeze through.

"Juniper's here, Dad! Jonathan too! They've come to see you."

The old man smiled, and more family members squeezed to the side to allow us to come through. An old woman patted me on the back and whispered, "Thank you for coming." We stayed well past the time we agreed to. We were so welcomed by family that we simply lost track of time. Juniper and Jonathan's dad walked us to the car. Just as we finished buckling the car seats, he said in a strained voice, "Thank you for coming, and…" He paused. "Thank you for always telling us about their medications and stuff…" He paused again and looked at his shoes. "Their mom can't read, and I'm not very good at it. We don't really understand what's going on."

I started to cry, and Mike reached around me and shook Dad's hand. "It's okay, man. No problem at all."

Our car ride home was silent. The world around us had shifted in an hour and a half. This family was kind, hardworking, and welcoming. They were at a disadvantage, and we suddenly knew that our role was not to just care for the kids but to advocate for the family as well.

8

WELCOMING FRIENDS

O ur wedding anniversary is the last day of July. Mike and I typically celebrate by going out to dinner or spending the night at a local bed-and-breakfast. This year, Mike and I were up to our ears in children and had decided to celebrate our anniversary by inviting friends over for a cookout instead of going on a date. As the night of our party quickly approached, we realized we were long overdue for a good night with friends. During nap time, I took Jonathan with me to the store to buy the last of a long list of things we still needed for the party. Mike stayed home while the kids napped so he could tidy the kitchen and prepare the grill.

I swung Jonathan's car seat easily out of the car and into the shopping cart, and then I tucked the diaper bag into the basket and locked the car behind me. Unfolding the creased list, I smoothed it along the edge of the cart and congratulated myself for my preparedness. I made a mental note to find my former Girl Scout leader on Facebook and thank her.

We hadn't made it past the bags of precut carrots before Jonathan pooped. I laughed and placed the carrots on the shelf then took him back out to the car to change his diaper.

Laying his blanket across the bench seat, I swiftly fixed the situation. He giggled, and I blew a raspberry on his belly. I folded the diaper and wipe neatly and tucked them into a plastic shopping bag that I kept in the van for such an occasion. Just then, the cart started to roll away with the car seat in it. I scooped Jonathan under one arm and ran after the cart. We returned to the car. I wiped my hands with a clean wipe and squirted a bit of hand sanitizer onto my open palm. I buckled the baby back into the car seat and closed the door behind me. We returned to the store and completely forgot to get the carrots.

Jonathan was ready for a bottle by aisle two, and I pulled one out of the diaper bag. I held the bottle in his mouth with one hand while glancing at my watch. A lot more time had passed than I'd thought. I vowed to move a little faster. Pushing the cart with one hand and feeding the baby with the other, I navigated the aisles with efficiency. I stopped every few minutes to burp him, but I still felt good about my efforts at multitasking. Remembering that we were out of dog food, I steered toward the pet supplies. Jonathan had no intention of finishing his bottle in less than an hour, and I propped it up with a burp cloth while I retrieved the large bag of food from the shelf.

"You know you should never prop a baby's bottle, right?"

The voice came from behind me. I was so surprised I dropped the bag of food, instinctively reaching for the cart. I pulled it closer to me and looked up. A woman in her midforties was standing close to Jonathan with her arms folded. I saw her sleek galoshes slipped neatly over her leggings. The leggings retailed for $55 at a boutique, and the boots were nearly $200. It was a trend that felt a little off in the blistering heat of our suburban neighborhood. I fought the urge to point this out to her and instead unfolded my body to meet her height. It was one of the rare moments I cursed my short stature.

I fixed my face and posture to what I believed was a no-nonsense stance. She wagged a finger at me, and I took a step closer to Jonathan. She took a step back. I pushed the cart away while biting my tongue and left the bag of dog food on the floor. The woman kept admonishing me while I turned the corner and walked toward the checkout.

Jonathan started whimpering as I unloaded the groceries onto the belt, and I held him to my shoulder, burping him while the teenager at the cash register scanned the items in what I was sure at the time was the slowest possible manner. She reached the cases of beer and bottles of wine I bought for the party and had to call for someone older to run the order. By then, Jonathan was really crying. I soothed and shushed him, oblivious to the change of cashier. "ID, please," the older woman said in a flat tone. I looked up with surprise. "Oh, okay. Of course, sorry about that." I fumbled with the diaper bag and the fussy baby. I felt my temperature rising and cursed myself for not putting the wallet in a more accessible place. With one hand I dug past the changes of clothes, June's medical supplies, and a few snack packs I'd placed in there for Aaron. Finally, my hand grazed the zipper of my wallet, and I breathed a sigh of relief. I handed the cashier my ID and waited.

"Having a party?" she asked in a dry tone.

"Yes, it's an anniversary party," I replied with much less enthusiasm than I had felt an hour ago. I put a whimpering Jonathan back in his car seat and pushed the haul toward the van.

I pushed the cart close to the van and propped a door open to secure the cart from rolling again. As soon as I opened the door, a wave of heat came billowing out, and also something putrid. My hand flew to my forehead, and I said, "Oh no!" A man in the car next to me whipped around and made a cough of surprise.

"Are you okay?" He moved toward me with concern.

"Don't come closer…sorry, yes, I'm okay." I shook my head and began to laugh again. "I forgot a poopy diaper in the van. It surprised me, that's all."

He laughed too and backed away with mock fear. "Good luck with that," he shouted over his shoulder.

I disposed of the diaper, loaded the car, and buckled Jonathan in. I drove toward home with the windows rolled down and the air conditioner blasting in hopes of clearing the air.

At home, Mike was putting charcoal in the grill when he heard the doorbell ring. Assuming it was neighborhood kids, he went back to his task. On the third ring, he flung the back door open with a little too much force and walked quickly to the front door with plans to send the neighbors home until the party. He turned the handle to find Ms. Hopkins with her hand hovering over the doorbell, poised to ring one more time. Mike's surprise to see her standing there was evident.

"Hello. May I come in?" she made the request in her usual even tone.

"Sure, of course…come on in," Mike replied, allowing her to move past him.

"I'll need you to show me to the children. As you know, I need to see them each month. Where are they?" she continued in her dry tone.

"Jonathan is with my wife, and Juniper is taking her nap," Mike answered, showing her to the kitchen. "We can wait in here if you would like." Mike picked up the phone to call me, but as soon as he pressed the send button, the phone buzzed across the counter.

Ms. Hopkins surely had a first name, but I don't think anyone knew it. She insisted on being called Ms. Hopkins and did not welcome any personal interaction or connectedness with the children

or families she supervised. She executed each home visit with efficiency, and this time was no different. She sighed when Mike could
not locate me but went straight to her work. Her list included checking for running water, flushing the toilets, and checking the refrigerator for food. She turned the handle on the kitchen faucet, noting
that there was no hot water. She turned and raised a brow in Mike's
direction.

Ever the peacemaker, Mike replied with a smile and small laugh.
"Plumbing isn't our gift. The hot and cold are backward—try the
other side." She did but did not return the laugh. She moved swiftly
to the refrigerator, and looking over the top of her glasses, she
scanned the nearly empty shelves and made a note on her clipboard.
Mike felt anxious as he began to explain about the party and the fact
that I was at the grocery store at that very moment. She moved to
the bathroom and flushed the toilet. To Mike's relief, there was no
sign of the clog of Matchbox cars from the previous week. June was
obsessed with the toilet, and consequently, we had paid almost $300
in the last month to a plumber who now knew us by name.

Ms. Hopkins sat at the kitchen table to finish her paperwork
while Mike stood by awkwardly, watching. Aaron peeked around
the corner to ask if rest time was over. Christine and Grace were not
far behind. Christine always picked up on the emotional climate.
She looked from Ms. Hopkins to her dad and back. Then she turned
toward the sink, surveying the lunch mess. She began to load dishes
into the dishwasher. Aaron saw his opportunity to play unsupervised and bolted out the back door.

He was pretty good about staying in the backyard, but Mike
called after him anyway. "Stay right there on the play set, okay?"
Aaron nodded without looking back. Grace grabbed a book and sat
on the couch closest to the kitchen.

Ms. Hopkins glanced at her watch. "Do you know how long

your wife will be?" Mike replied that he did not know, which was not a satisfying answer. "You know I need to see the children every month. I don't have all day."

Before Mike could filter his answer, he met her even tone. "You probably should have called or made arrangements before the last day of the month."

The air grew thicker than the 100 percent humidity that loomed outside. Ms. Hopkins stood without response and made her way toward the stairs. "I'll look in on Juniper now." Mike wanted to scream for her to stop, knowing that June was one of the lightest sleepers he had ever known. A small creak of the door, and nap time would be over. As soon as the doorknob turned, June wailed. Ms. Hopkins entered the room and lifted the child from her bed. Juniper was not a fan of being carried and began to claw at the caseworker's face. Her arms and legs pushed with fierce resistance all the way down the stairs. Ms. Hopkins placed her on the floor and reached up to readjust her outfit and hair. Mike swung June up onto his shoulders—a trick that made her giggle. Just then, he heard my car pull into the driveway.

I nearly missed the red Honda parked in front of my house as I whipped my van into its parking space. I unbuckled Jonathan and grabbed a case of drinks with my other hand. Juggling the baby in one arm and the drinks in another, I made my way up the walk and burst through the front door, nearly barreling over Ms. Hopkins. "Oh!" I shouted in surprise. I had assumed all the children would still be resting but noted that the time was much later than I anticipated. I made eye contact with Mike and widened my eyes to communicate my shock. He shrugged his shoulders. Ms. Hopkins looked at Jonathan, thanked me for my time, and exited out the still open front door. Mike let out the breath he had been holding for the last hour.

I placed Jonathan on the floor, still in his car seat. June needed her feeding, and Aaron had been unsupervised for long enough to get in trouble. We herded the kids into the family room and put a cartoon on for them so we could gather our thoughts. We moved quickly to manage feeding supplies, groceries, diaper changes, and snacks for the big kids. Christine finished the dishes and curled up on the couch next to Grace, who was contentedly holding Jonathan. Aaron plopped down on a floor pillow. Juniper bounced in her Jenny Jump Up, a hot-pink seat strapped to a large bungee cord that was secured to the doorframe, and quite possibly my favorite invention of all time. Mike and I went out to the car to grab the rest of the groceries.

As we loaded our arms, I asked, "What just happened here?"

Mike propped one arm on the door while the other swung a gallon of milk aimlessly. "I always thought you were exaggerating about that caseworker. I'm embarrassed to say…I thought you were just…you know, oversensitive." I raised my eyebrows in a gesture that was meant to say "I told you so." I didn't speak, though, and let him tell the whole uncomfortable thing.

We both agreed to shake off the afternoon and focus on the party. That night, our friends arrived with full arms. They streamed into our home, dropping diaper bags at the door, organizing plates of food in the kitchen, and guiding children to the fenced-in yard. We had a sprinkler going, and Aaron had it positioned to hit the play set slide every few seconds. Our kids, who were already soaked to the bone, called out to their friends. A small baby pool was on the patio, and soon toddlers and moms hovered around it with cold drinks in hand.

Many of our friends were foster families as well, which led to a natural ease when it came to child supervision and flexibility. It wasn't unusual for one of us to show up to a get-together with a few extra children in tow. On this day, our good friends had a teen-ager and her newborn daughter with them. They were both strik-ingly beautiful and quite shy. Megan introduced Sadie to all of us, and in turn, Sadie introduced Giselle. "Oh," I gasped, "I love that ballet!" Sadie looked confused. I awkwardly explained that Giselle was the first ballet I had ever seen and that I loved it even though it was tragically sad. Sadie continued to half listen while scanning the crowded backyard.

Later, as the conversation lulled, I observed the young mother feeding her child and looking completely lost. I couldn't imagine what it would be like to enter foster care as a teen, much less with one foot in adulthood and still powerless to control my own future.

The kids played until the lightning bugs came out. Christine helped the little kids get jelly jars from the kitchen while I fed Juni-per in the family room. Grace and Aaron had a bet going about who could collect the most fireflies. "Can I keep them in my room, Mom?" they asked in unison.

"Just for one night, then you have to let them go," I replied, grateful that the two of them were not just brother and sister but also good friends. All the adults unfolded portable cribs and unrolled sleeping bags, preparing places for children to rest. The children brought jars filled with tiny blinking lights inside and crawled into cozy spots. Sadie and Giselle settled into our playroom, where we had an extra TV and a comfy couch. I knew Sadie must be over-whelmed by the newness of this rowdy crew. She curled up on the couch with her baby in her arms and smiled as she set her own jar of lightning bugs on the end table.

That night, we stayed up until well past midnight, laughing and talking around the campfire, each parent taking turns checking on the kids. The neighbor peeked over the fence to shush us, and though we apologized profusely, we roared with laughter moments later. Moving inside, we attempted to wrap up our visit, only to pull out more snacks and stories. We laughed till we cried. Aaron padded into the kitchen to ask us to be quiet, and we stifled another round of laughter as Mike returned him to his bed with a promise that the moms and dads would whisper.

Finally, we carried blanketed children to car seats, loaded trunks with casserole dishes, and waved goodbye to our friends. Mike and I straightened furniture, folded small blankets, and rinsed the last of the dishes. We marveled at the success of the night and our good fortune at finding such good friends. We swept the last of the crumbs and took out the trash. The house looked as if the party had never happened.

As we climbed the stairs toward our room, I turned back to look at our recently emptied home. It still felt full, the echo of laughter quietly ringing in my ears, and I smiled. We checked each child, kissed foreheads, and retucked blankets. I fed June one more time while rocking in the chair next to her crib. When I finally crawled into our bed that night, I let out my own satisfied sigh. It had been too long since we had spent the evening with friends. I draped my arm over my softly snoring husband and promised not to let that much time pass again. My head hit the pillow knowing that June's and Jonathan's next feedings were coming soon.

Part 3

THE CHANGE
OF AUTUMN

9

WIDENING THE CIRCLE

June and Jonathan's mom and dad started doing visits in our home in early August. Their caseworker was hesitant at first, but the judge assigned to the case didn't see any reason visits couldn't take place under our supervision. The plan was still reunification, and with more medical information being added to their file each week, the children's failure to thrive was considered likely to be a medical condition instead of the previously believed neglect.

Mike spoke up in court on behalf of Mom and Dad. During each hearing, every party present was given an opportunity to add anything they deemed necessary. This was our very brief chance to advocate for the children. As foster parents, we had the unique perspective of seeing both Mom and Dad as well as the children. We knew the level of care the children needed each day, and we also knew that Mom and Dad couldn't understand much of what doctors had been telling them.

We wondered if the presence of an intellectual disability was really a reason for someone not to parent. They were clearly loving, kind, hardworking, and filled with joy, and they delighted in their children. But they had difficulty understanding the instructions on the bottle of phenobarbital, a medication June took to control her seizures. I myself found I had to read and reread them each time I measured a dose, and I had a college education, a typical IQ, and plenty of resources to help me. I wondered out loud how Mom and Dad were going to manage the medications and feeding schedule at home. They had the desire to parent but not the resources. The day Mike spoke up in court, our view on our purpose in the foster-care system began to shift again.

On the drive home from court, we recounted our most recent victory. Mom and Dad would be able to visit in our home. That meant much more time for us to coach them on the medications, feeding schedule, and NG placement. Each of these skills would be assessed by the caseworker in the coming weeks. She would make a report to the judge to determine the direction of this case. Reunification is always the plan for children in foster care. In this case, the plan hadn't been changed, but the new information about the children's medical diagnoses weighed heavily on the court's determination of whether the children needed to be in care at all. The team surrounding June and Jonathan began to consider the idea that the children might have been removed without proper consideration for all aspects of their care. It was possible that the children might have been able to stay in the home if only Mom and Dad had been given support in the first place.

This idea plagued us as well. We had begun to adjust to our family of seven, and we loved Juniper and Jonathan. But even as we looked at them with love, we had to admit that they were not ours to keep. They had a mom and dad who missed them each day and loved them more than anything. I walked through the house the night after we got back from court and kissed each of my sleeping children.

Visits began the day after. Christine, Grace, and Aaron were at day camp when June and Jonathan's mom and dad showed up. Dad had taken the morning off work, something we knew he couldn't afford to do. Mike was at work, and I was home alone with the children. I welcomed them cheerfully at the door.

Dad stood on the front steps wide-eyed. "Are you rich?" he said before he could take the words back.

I coughed in surprise and surveyed my home from his perspective. I guess it did look expensive. I was so used to living in the wealthiest county in Indiana, I had forgotten how the rest of the world lives. We had, by far, one of the more modest incomes in the area, and I was used to the judgmental look we got whenever the kids invited friends over. This was new for me, and I was humbled that anyone would think of me as rich. I shook off the realization and turned toward the task at hand. Supervised visits. My supervised visits.

We didn't have much time if they were going to master all the skills they needed by the next time everyone involved in the children's care met for a "team meeting." We began with tube feedings. I secured the mesh gate across the opening to the family room and then laid the feeding supplies on a tray on the floor next to the blanket. "Okay, who wants to go first?" Mom and Dad exchanged glances. "I know—it looks worse than it is. I promise. Did I ever tell you about the first time I had to do this?" I told them all about the nurses and the near fainting episode, which was not my most shining moment.

They laughed, and the tension was eased. Dad volunteered, so I placed Jonathan on Mom's lap. She held him loosely and without confidence. I noticed she was sneaking looks at my face every few seconds, presumably to see if I was watching. "Okay, the first step is to get June-Bug to come over here," I proclaimed with a half laugh. "And that's usually the hardest part!"

Dad froze. "My grandpa always called her June-Bug." I watched as his eyes filled with tears. I turned away, not wanting to embarrass him.

"Is that okay? I mean, is it okay that we call her that? I didn't know…I'm sorry," I whispered.

"No, of course it's okay. We love it. My grandpa held our family together, you know? It's been hard without him here," Dad replied.

Mom bounced Jonathan on her knees and smiled at him. "JuneBug…I like it." I wasn't sure if she was talking to me or herself or just some emptiness in the room. Dad called Juniper to the blanket. She raced toward him and flung her little body into her father's arms. He squeezed her with delight. I vowed then and there to do everything I could to support them as a family.

June allowed herself to be wrapped in the blanket by her dad. I explained how to tuck the corners in. He placed the NG tube without too much hesitation and measured her formula into the tube. We carefully pulled the tube and practiced a second time. Mom watched from the couch but made no move to help. She decided she was too nervous to try on her own but agreed to give it a go on the next visit. Dad completed the feeding, but as the formula slowly dripped down the tube, he admitted that he was worried about following each step when he was alone. I offered to write it down before realizing that he struggled with reading. Silence filled the air.

"Well, it looks like you guys have this under control. I'm going to do the dishes." I excused myself to the kitchen. After I loaded the dishwasher, Dad indicated that June was done with her feeding. I came back into the family room and helped remove the tube, and then I invited Mom and Dad into the kitchen to clean her equipment. Our faucet had been dripping for a month, and the irritating sound had become nothing but background noise to me.

After placing the equipment on the counter, Dad pointed to the sink. "I can fix that, you know."

I turned and looked at Mom. "Really?"

Mom nodded. "Yeah, he's a plumber." Dad asked for my permission first and tools second. I was so embarrassed for him to see how we kept our toolbox. Without an ounce of judgment, he took the box to the kitchen and fixed the dripping sink. When he returned the tools, he carefully organized the entire box before returning it to the garage. Normally I hated the way mechanically minded people made me feel inadequate, but his attitude was one of dignity and respect.

"Thanks! Seriously—thanks!" I was so happy to have the sink fixed.

We all stood in the kitchen admiring the dripless sink when June made a noise that surely meant "Look at me!" And we did. She peeked over the mesh gate in a game of peekaboo. When Mom smiled at her, she ducked beneath the bar and then pressed her face into the mesh, stretching her skin flat across it. The three adults burst into laughter, and so did June. She persisted with the game until it was time for me to get the big kids from camp. I couldn't believe how quickly time had flown. Mom and Dad carried the kids to my van and helped get them buckled in.

"Let's set the visit around your schedule next time. I know you guys have to work. I can be pretty flexible during the summer," I offered. They agreed to call that night with their schedule and set up a time.

They returned a few nights later when the entire family was home. We set the family room up for them to visit and practice and sent our older three to the playroom with some crafts. Mike stopped by the grocery on the way home from work and bought a few frozen pizzas. Mom and Dad settled in a little more quickly this time, and I could tell the kids could feel the relaxed nature of their parents.

Dad began, "I was thinking about the way I learned plumbing.

I watched other people and could remember what they did like watching a video in my mind. I was thinking, could we record all the things we need to do with the kids, and then maybe we could watch it at home for practice?"

A grin spread across Mike's face. "Yes! I love the idea. I'll go get my phone." If there is one thing I love about Mike, it is his enthusiasm for creative solutions to problems. Mom and I gathered medications and feeding supplies from the kitchen, and Dad got Jonathan and Juniper settled into the family room.

Mike returned with his phone and a full-blown plan for our video session. Mom, Dad, and I joked about our acting skills and then got to work. Mom was still nervous about all of June's many supplies. I sympathized. I would sometimes lie awake at night quizzing myself on seizure meds and feeding supplies. Mike recorded the entire procedure, start to finish. Then he recorded Mom measuring each medication. By the time we were finished, we had about 30 minutes of short videos. At the beginning of each, I looked at the camera and stated the name of what we were about to do next. "This is a syringe…This is phenobarbital…We give it at seven p.m. Here is how we measure phenobarbital." I felt a little silly talking to the camera. I think Mom and Dad felt silly at first too, but they did each task beautifully. When we were done, their footage was the best.

We edited the videos that night and sent them through an email to Mom and Dad before we went to bed. "You know what? That was fun," Mike said as he clicked out the light.

"I agree. I can't believe no one thought of that before," I marveled. "You know, when Dad fixed the sink the other day, he didn't make me feel stupid. I appreciated that so much. I hope that when we are fostering, we never make people feel small."

Mike rolled over and looked me in the eye. "I think we learned the wrong thing about ministry, you know? We were taught that we are here to bring something to the less fortunate, that we have all the answers. I always sort of thought that others were small and we were big. Now I feel different. The families we work with don't have to like us. In fact, they have every reason to hate us. June and Jonathan's mom and dad are nice to us, and they don't have to be. I think maybe God wants us to love one another and allow others to love us the way He does. I don't know if that makes sense." He yawned.

"It does." I yawned too, and we fell asleep fully aware that June's feeding would come soon.

Mom and Dad watched the videos with determination, and when they returned a few days later, they completed each task with efficiency. Our team meeting was one week away, and I knew we would be saying goodbye soon.

Meanwhile, the hospital threw a curveball at us. They wanted Juniper to have a G-tube placed because her eating had not improved and the NG tube was not a long-term solution. It was an easy surgery, but it was going to fall right at the time that in-home visits at Mom and Dad's were to begin. We attended the team meeting and sat back while Mom and Dad explained their new plan for caring for the kids. In a short time, they had gone from displaying insecurity to showing confidence as they advocated for their children and themselves. The team agreed that in-home visits should start immediately. I went home and packed a bag for each child.

Mike stayed with Christine and Aaron while Grace and I drove the little ones to their visit. She was most attached to the kids and needed to see where they were going to live. We took the highway for about 30 minutes until we reached our exit, followed by a series of smaller side streets. We found the tiny brick home at the end of a narrow dead-end street. There were four cars in the driveway, and I had barely enough room to turn my van. I stepped out of the van and right into a puddle. Warning Grace to stay put, I made my way through the mud to her door. I lifted her over the puddle and onto the sidewalk and then unbuckled both of the younger children. They squirmed—June with recognition as she reached for the familiar home. Grace held on to the diaper bag while navigating the mud. I seemed incapable of avoiding it and finally soaked myself up to the ankle.

Mom and Dad met us at the door and invited us into the house. We squeezed through the narrowly open door and discovered that a stack of boxes was preventing it from opening all the way. More boxes lined the small entryway. We filed individually between the boxes until we reached the family room. The television was blaring, and I found it difficult to hear. They invited us to sit on the couch, and we did. An ashtray on the side table next to the sofa held a cigarette, which still emitted a small swirl of smoke. Grace, who is asthmatic, glanced at the cigarette with a worried expression. The room was clean but filled with stuff. Toys, newspapers, and baskets of clean laundry covered every inch of carpet. June and Jonathan seemed relaxed and happy, and the family looked complete. We made plans to meet the following day and said goodbye.

Grace and I returned less gingerly to the car than when we came in. We accepted that the rain would soak our clothes, knowing we would dry on the way home. Sliding into our seats, we slipped off our shoes and clicked our seat belts.

Grace looked at me and said, "Is it okay?"

I was confused. "Is what okay, sweetie?"

She paused and then answered, "The house—is it okay to live like that? I mean, is it safe?"

I could understand her hesitation. I felt the same way. It was messy and cluttered, and the smoke concerned me. When I really thought about it though, there were no actual hazards that I could see. Outlets were covered. No sharp objects. It was just different.

"I think it's going to be just fine. All families have different ways of living. Their home is good because their mom and dad are there." Grace accepted this answer, and once I said it out loud, I did too.

In-home visits increased over the next few weeks leading up to the appointment for June's G-tube. They were going well, and it was easy to be excited for the family to get back together. At night though, when the kids were all asleep and the house was quiet, I would lift Jonathan out of his crib for his 2:00 a.m. feeding and hold him close to me. Rocking in that same chair where I rocked my other children, I whispered to his sleepy face, "I love you. I'll always love you. Mommy loves you. Daddy loves you. Mike loves you. Kristin loves you. Brothers and sisters love you. Grandmas and grandpas love you. Jesus loves you." His tiny eyelashes fluttered and then rested as I breathed in the baby scent of his peach-fuzz hair. Something caught in my throat, and I quickly kissed him and gently put him back into his crib.

I took Juniper to the hospital on a Thursday. The big kids were just starting back to school, so Mike stayed home long enough to get them on the bus while I took the little kids to the hospital. Jonathan was patient and sat happily in his stroller while I filled out paperwork and wrestled June back into the lobby approximately 200 times. Mom and Dad were late, and I was beginning to get frazzled. Finally, they called Juniper to come back. Mom and Dad rushed in the door just in time. Mom was wearing pajama pants, and I started to judge her before admonishing myself with the reminder that people are different. Besides, I hadn't bothered to look in a mirror that morning either, so who was I to judge?

Mom and Dad invited me to stay with them while June was in surgery. I did. Family members showed up in droves. They seemed to come out of the woodwork. We all waited in the lobby together, passing the baby from one relative to another and drinking up all the hospital's crummy coffee. Finally, the surgery was complete. A relative offered to watch Jonathan so all three of us could go back. I agreed.

June was groggy, which was such an unusual state for her that it was hard to recognize her. The doctor gave us an update, Mom and Dad settled in, and it was almost time for me to get my big kids off the bus. I kissed June and told Mom and Dad goodbye. The court had approved for Mom and Dad to stay with June at the hospital while I kept Jonathan for a day or two until things were settled at home. I retrieved the baby from his great aunt and made the long trek out to my van.

That night, the big kids made cards for June and helped me pack the rest of her and Jonathan's things. It was bittersweet to see them put so much care into their little brother and sister. We loaded the boxes, totes, and toys into the car so I could drop them off at Mom and Dad's house the following day. The plan was for them to take both children home once Mom and Dad learned to care for the G-tube and give feedings.

The caseworker called the next day around noon. I thought it was the call to take the children home. I felt a mixture of sadness and excitement as I answered the phone. "Mrs. Berry, this is Ms. Hopkins. Mom and Dad are having difficulty accomplishing the proper placement of Juniper's G-tube. We had an emergency team meeting this morning to discuss a solution. You will need to get Juniper from the hospital today, and Jonathan can leave with them. You will need to be there at three."

I nearly dropped the phone before answering. "My kids get off the bus at three; I can't be there at that time."

Ms. Hopkins sighed, and I felt my anger rising. This disregard for the lives of others made my blood boil. I opened my mouth to respond when she said, "I'm sorry this happened. I know it's frustrating. I will call the hospital to see if she can be discharged to you in an hour."

I stifled my anger and thanked her. I grabbed Jonathan and buckled him into his car seat and walked next door to see if the neighbor could get my children off the bus if I ended up running late. She agreed. We made good time on the drive, and before I had time to process the change, I was holding Jonathan in the elevator and pushing the button for the top floor. The doors swished shut, and the reality that the baby was leaving hit me. He snuggled close to my chest, and I whispered, "I love you. I love you. I love you." Tears streamed down my cheeks and onto his soft baby head. I kissed him once, and the doors breezed open. Wiping my tears, I righted myself and walked toward Juniper's room. I entered the room to find Mom and Dad playing with June in a pile of colorful toys that had been donated by various organizations. June looked happy.

Mom and Dad looked up, and Dad spoke first. "We couldn't figure it out."

My own sadness momentarily forgotten, I replied, "I know. You know what, though? You thought you wouldn't learn the other stuff, but you did! So we'll just do the same as we did last time."

Mom spoke up. "I'm disappointed." I could see it etched across her face.

"I know. But it's just a tiny bump in the road. You will work this out, and before long, all this will be a memory." It was true. All this would just be a memory for all of us soon.

The doctors released Juniper to me at 1:45 p.m., leaving plenty of time for me to help Mom and Dad load Jonathan's stuff into their car and to drive my own half-empty van straight home to get my children. I parked my van in the driveway just before the bus pulled into the neighborhood. I opened the door to take June out of the car as Aaron ran up the driveway. He froze when he saw her and dropped his jaw. He threw his bag onto the driveway and ran into the house slamming the door. Grace and Christine looked confused as they watched me unbuckle June.

"I thought we said goodbye last night," Christine questioned.

I shrugged my shoulders. "We are going to get to spend a few more days with June-Bug." Christine smiled, and so did Grace.

Over the next two weeks, Mom and Dad came over every chance they could. They practiced June's medications and feedings and watched themselves on video at home. At the team meeting, they found out that a court order had been placed for them to take Juniper home immediately. Everyone smiled. I cried, of course. They followed us to our car, loaded the rest of Juniper's things, and hugged us goodbye. We promised to stay in touch. As Mike and I drove home, I glanced at the empty car seat in my rearview mirror and wondered who would walk through our doors next.

10

NOT EMPTY FOR LONG

We slept soundly for the first time in months the night Juniper and Jonathan left. Aaron woke us at 6:30 a.m. He climbed up my side of the bed and planted a grimy palm right on my mouth. I jolted awake, thinking something was wrong. I pushed Aaron aside and leaped from bed, groping around for my glasses on the carpet. I located them and turned toward Jonathan's bed, thinking for a moment that I had forgotten to feed him during the night. The realization hit me when I saw the empty crib. I turned to see Aaron's confused face.

"I just wanted to snuggle." He turned away from me and curled closer to Mike.

I smiled—he hadn't done this in years. I climbed back in bed, placing my glasses carefully on the nightstand. I wrapped my arms around him and squeezed. "Hey, you took my pillow! Don't you dare drool on it."

He giggled. "I will, you know I will." Then he closed his eyes and went back to sleep.

Breakfast was an adjustment of a different kind. We were so used to spending hours feeding, medicating, and supervising. We hadn't had a quiet breakfast in months. We all sat at the breakfast table together and said goodbye as Mike left for work. Everyone was dressed, cereal bowls were washed, and backpacks were packed by eight. School didn't start for another hour! Christine suggested we stop at the donut shop.

We had plenty of time to go to our favorite one. Simply called "Donuts," it's run by an elderly man who wakes up bright and early each morning (except Sundays) and makes donuts. When the donuts have been placed neatly in the display case, he turns the sign on the front door to announce that he is open. He accepts only cash, and when the donuts are sold out, he turns the sign to read closed. I was already late by Donuts' standards. A few older men remained in the seating area, gathered around small square tables, reading sections of the newspaper. The four of us filed in and went straight to the display case. There were about 15 donuts left. "Just in time," the owner said with a smile.

Aaron pointed a tiny finger at the one he wanted and said, "This one, please." I marveled at his small hands. They still looked like baby hands, with tiny dimples on the knuckles. I wondered for a second when they would change. What is that magical moment when a child loses that softness? I had missed it with my girls. I vowed to watch him closely each day. I didn't want to miss a minute.

Lost in thought, I didn't realize that the owner was talking to me. "I haven't seen you in a while?" he said as a statement and a question.

I snapped to attention and registered what he had said. "We've had our hands full for the past few months. We missed these donuts though!" I replied. Grace and Christine chose vanilla and chocolate frosted, respectively. We returned to the car with our treats and agreed that there was still time to go to the park.

Aaron couldn't wait to get to the park to eat his donut, and neither could I! I licked the sticky sweetness off each finger as we pulled into the parking lot. I glanced at Aaron, who was wearing most of the icing. After parking, I handed him a wipe. We walked the familiar trails, playing a game we often played at the park. It was like follow the leader, but the leader changes with each direction. If Aaron directed us to go left at the oak tree, then Christine might direct us to go right at the swings, and Grace might lead us straight into the creek. The time went by quickly, and soon it was time to go to school.

Foster care had been an adventure, but it was nice to be with our children for some uninterrupted time. As I dropped them off outside the elementary school, I wondered how long it would be before another child needed a place to stay.

I stopped at the car wash before heading to the grocery store. The last few weeks had taken a toll on our pantry, and I was looking forward to making something healthy for dinner. The sign on the vacuum said two dollars for eight minutes. Nearly thirty minutes and six dollars later, I finally swept up the last cheerio and stood back to admire my work. Just as I was about to shut the heavy door, I saw something soft and pink peek out from beneath the driver's seat. I climbed back into the car and crawled under the seat, reaching my arm as far as it would go. I couldn't see what I was grabbing at but wiggled my fingers to loosen the object. Finally, it came free, and I gripped it with my thumb and forefinger. It was Juniper's shoe. Tears welled up as I thought about her running to grab that pair of pretty pink shoes every time we got ready to go somewhere. She never kept them on past the end of our driveway though and delighted in flinging them off her feet as soon as I turned the key in the ignition. I missed her. I tucked her shoe in my purse and drove toward the grocery store.

I had more neglected errands than I could complete in one day and had to return home in time for the bus to arrive. The kids came home as always—with too much homework and way too much energy to sit down and complete it. We fell back into our typical routine easily, but the day still felt uncomfortably empty. That night, Mike and I put the kids to bed, and I left to meet up with friends at Target. I still had some errands to run and hadn't had time with friends in a while. It was my version of killing two birds with one stone. Mike planned to go out with his friends the following night. It felt good to get back to a somewhat normal routine. My friends and I met up at the "good" Target. It was a little farther from my house, but it always had a better selection of things I wasn't looking for and didn't need. I unfolded my list and began getting the necessities before browsing and talking, which was the actual reason for the trip.

My phone rang just as I reached the family-size rolls of toilet paper. I stopped midreach and answered.

"Hello, is this Kristin Berry?" a woman's voice asked.

"Yes, this is she," I replied, just as Mrs. Shearer, my eighth-grade English teacher, taught me.

"This is Andréa from Department of Child Services. I understand you may have an opening in your home. Are you able to pick a baby up tonight from the office? He is 12 weeks old. We don't have any details yet about how long it will be, but we don't have anyone else tonight."

I glanced at my friends and then answered, "Yes, I will be there in about 40 minutes. Does he have anything with him?"

She let me know that he did not have anything. She knew he was on Enfamil formula and was currently wearing a size 1 diaper. I thanked her and hung up the phone. I almost forgot to get the toilet paper, but Nicole gestured to the nearly forgotten item while shaking her head. Nicole and Megan helped me gather just the essentials to get me through the night. Then I remembered I left my car seat at home. Nicole agreed to allow me to borrow hers.

I made a quick call to Mike to let him know what was going on. He was already asleep, but I could hear the TV in the background. I felt a little bad for him. He loves sports documentaries and usually waited until I was gone to watch them. Just one of the many loving marital compromises he made for me every day, and now he had fallen asleep during his chance to watch one completely alone without my unappreciated commentary in the background. He woke up quickly when I told him what was going on. I could hear the hesitancy in his voice, but he agreed that we would fulfill this commitment.

I arrived at the office just before 9:30 p.m. Andréa sat on the couch in the lobby and watched me arrive. I pulled the van close to the door, not bothering to park in the empty parking lot. I walked toward the locked door, but I didn't even have to knock. The case-worker turned the lock to let me inside. I followed her to look at the sleeping child, who had been placed on a blanket on the floor of the office. He was beautiful.

"His name is Gabe, we think. Neighbors made the call this afternoon after hearing the child crying for hours. They hadn't seen any adults go in or out of the home for hours. The police were able to unlock the door, but we have not been able to locate a parent. We've been looking all day. He was inside alone. I really don't know more than that. I'm sorry."

I looked at her face as she recounted the story, still visibly shaken. I could tell she was young. "Well, we are flexible. Just let me know what you find out. He has a place for tonight."

She looked relieved, and I could sense that her emotions were about to get the best of her. She shook her head as if to regain her composure. "I will stop by tomorrow with his medical passport."

I nodded and scooped the baby up into my arms. He was so light, and he barely made a noise. He opened one tiny eye as if to size me up and then fell back to sleep. The caseworker followed me out of the door and turned to lock it behind her.

As I buckled Gabe into the car seat, I paused and reached my head back out the window. "You're doing a great job," I said before thinking it though.

She made a choking noise and simply said, "Thanks." Not all caseworkers were easy to work with—I knew that firsthand. Most were simply doing the best they could at a job that chipped away at their heart each day. I knew that firsthand too.

Gabe slept all the way home. I unbuckled his entire car seat and carried him inside. Nicole had already stopped by to grab my car seat so that she wouldn't be stuck the following morning. Mike was waiting up for me and helped me unload the car. I had purchased two tiny outfits, a box of diapers, and a canister of formula. I had all of Jonathan's stuff in a tote at the bottom of the basement stairs. I hadn't even stored it away yet. I fixed Gabe a bottle and attempted to feed him. I told Mike I would stay on the couch with Gabe for the night so that he could be well rested for an early day of work the next day. He agreed and kissed me quickly before heading to bed.

I set up the Pack 'n Play next to the couch and, after burping Gabe, placed him on the fitted sheet and fell asleep as soon as my own head hit the pillow. My alarm was set for three hours so I could wake up and check on him if necessary. He slept through that alarm, and I reset it again for 5:00 a.m. I woke to feed him, and then he fell asleep again. I still had two hours before the kids needed to be up for school. Mike said goodbye and crept out the front door without waking anyone else up.

Sleeping on the couch hadn't been as bad as I anticipated. I felt quite rested. Gabe woke up at 7:30, just as the kids were getting out of bed. I put him in the front carrier and went about my morning routine. Aaron was the first to wake, and he noticed Gabe right away. He always loved babies, so when I sat Gabe in the bouncy seat near the breakfast table, Aaron volunteered to entertain him. Grace and Christine were equally taken with Gabe. They all smiled and made faces at him throughout breakfast. Gabe seemed fascinated with them as well. He stared without expression, watching their every move.

The morning went smoothly. The kids had remembered to pack lunches the night before, so all they had to do was grab them from the fridge. I was proud of how efficient they were and told them so. Grace grinned with pride. "I did what you asked the first time." I gave her a high five and hugged all three as we heard the bus arrive on our block. The kids raced out the door, leaving me alone to care for Gabe.

The caseworker called by 9:30. She needed me to take Gabe to the doctor to document his weight, length, and overall health. I agreed and jotted the Medicaid number on a scrap piece of paper. The doctor was almost an hour away, so I called the office and explained the situation. The lady who answered seemed kind and understanding. She gave me the information I needed to know, and I prepared Gabe to make the trip. I glanced at the clock and realized that I was supposed to be at the dentist. I was pretty sure I had a cavity and wasn't in the mood to deal with it anyway, so I called and canceled before leaving the house.

Gabe and I made it to the doctor's office by 11:00. We waited in the crowded lobby for over an hour. When it was finally our turn, I walked up to the registration desk with Gabe cradled in my arms. I gave the Medicaid number and the letter from the Department of Child Services giving me permission to take him to the doctor.

The woman taking my registration must not have been the same lady who answered the phone. She sighed and looked over her glasses at me, sizing me up. She slowly punched in the numbers from his insurance card. She looked at her computer and then at me and again at Gabe. Then she said slowly, "I don't know why you think his name is Gabe. What are you trying to pull?" I paused before answering, and she took that as license to continue. "This Medicaid number is for Matthew Gabriel Jones."

I stopped myself from rolling my eyes in exasperation. "I'm going to guess that Gabriel is his middle name and that he goes by that—Gabriel, Gabe."

She sighed as if I were the one making a stupid mistake. "Fine," she replied. She made a big show of calling the Department of Child Services and asking for Andréa. This took another 15 minutes, and Gabe began to get fussy. I fumbled with the diaper bag and produced a bottle. He ate greedily. The lady continued to drone on, lecturing the caseworker about my paperwork. I found it difficult to hide my surprise that she had reached a caseworker. Finally, she was satisfied and gestured for me to wait again in the lobby. I did.

Another hour went by, and we were finally called back into the doctor's office. The nurses were kind, but my nerves were shot. I had so much work to do at home and kids returning from school shortly. This was always the downside to foster care. It was a full-time volunteer job. I silently stewed about the people I had heard in the past criticize foster parents for "doing it for the money." I frowned just thinking about it. Our typical stipend was about $17 a day, which wouldn't even cover the cost of a day care center. For the little one I now held in my arms, I had already spent close to $100 on formula, clothes, diapers, and gas that would never be reimbursed. I didn't mind, but sometimes I just wished others understood the sacrifice foster parents made every day.

The nurse made eye contact with me, and I noticed her confused expression. "Is everything okay?" she asked cautiously.

I snapped back to reality. "Oh, sorry! Yes, I'm fine. This is Gabe."

The nurse weighed him and measured him. She was familiar with the check that DCS required, and she swiftly went through her checklist of measurements. Then she carefully removed his outfit and looked over his body for any sign of physical abuse or neglect. She noted that he was underweight but looked quite healthy otherwise. She was concerned about some bites on his torso and near his neck. Thinking it might be fleas, she cautioned me to go home and wash everything. I raised my hand to my forehead, I hadn't even thought of that. She assured me that they did not look like bedbug bites, and I silently thanked the Lord for that small favor.

The doctor came in next. She was a beautiful, tall, regal-looking woman. I was surprised to find her in a clinic like this. She seemed so out of place standing next to the dingy walls. She looked him over as well and signed off on his evaluation. They printed off a copy for me and faxed another to the caseworker and then apologized for the time we had been waiting there. I found that I was not irritated. I understood. We shook hands, and I left the office, heading toward home and another day of homework, dishes, and managing another new normal.

11

SURPRISING CONNECTIONS

Gabe slept soundly for the second night in a row. It was a relief to have a child whose demands weren't as constant as the previous children. However, the relaxed nature of this child was almost unnerving. Mike and I continued to keep an eye on him for any signs of distress. The other children were thrilled to have a sweet baby to care for. Aaron talked about Gabe constantly, and Grace set about the task of fixing formula and washing bottles. Christine always enjoyed the bigger kids a little more, but even she couldn't resist stopping by his baby swing for a quick game of peekaboo. We didn't hear anything from his caseworker for three more days. Finally, she came to visit on the fourth day, bringing all the information she had been able to gather. It wasn't much. We found out that his parents had been arrested on the day Gabe was left home alone. They had attempted to buy drugs from an undercover police officer. Upon their arrest, they made no mention of the child. If it hadn't been for the neighbor's call, Gabe may have been alone for days—or worse.

I could tell that Andréa was deeply affected by Gabe's story. She remained professional as she recounted the details, but her voice cracked. I resisted the urge to hug her and only gave her a half smile. I bounced Gabe on my knee one more time and then handed him to her. She took him and gave him a squeeze.

"For what it's worth, I know this job is hard. I know there are times you question yourself. This is not one of those times. You did the right thing here. Look at him. He's fine." I hoped I hadn't said too much.

She just nodded and handed him back. She told me she had been looking for relatives for the past few days but had found no one to take kinship care yet. She wanted to know if we were okay if this went long-term. I said that we were fine with that.

Andréa left, and as I closed the door behind her, I turned to see Christine. Tears flowed freely, and her tiny fists were clenched.

"Oh no!" I exclaimed. "How much of that did you hear?" She opened her mouth and then shut it again. Opened and then shut and then glared at me. I was confused but moved toward her to hug her. Her arms went rigid at her side, and her body language pushed me away even though she physically did not move. I rushed to put Gabe down and return to Christine. I was too late, and she was already in her room with the door closed. I knocked, and she ignored me. I knocked again. I pressed my ear to the door and knocked softly one more time. A piece of paper slipped out under the door. "Go AWAY!" it read.

I braced myself before answering. "It's okay to be upset. I can talk to you in a bit." She still ignored me. I went to my room and grabbed a pen. I took her sheet of paper and wrote, "I love you, I'm going to go downstairs and fix a snack. We can talk when you're ready."

She wasn't ready to talk until bedtime. As I tucked her blanket around her, she ducked under the sheets. "My mom left me too." I lifted the blanket to look at her eyes. They were scrunched shut.

"I'm sorry that happened, Christine. I know you feel sad." She nodded and opened her eyes just enough to look at me beneath her lashes. "Is it okay if I say the prayer tonight?" I asked. She nodded again. "Father, thank You for protecting Gabe when his mom and dad couldn't be there. Thank You for protecting Christine when her mom and dad couldn't be there too. We know You created Christine with a purpose and a plan. We know You knew just the right two people to make her. She is just perfect. Thank You. Amen." I kissed her forehead.

"Goodnight, Mommy," she whispered.

After the kids were asleep, Mike fed Gabe, and I grabbed a snack and the remote. We chose a show, but before we started watching, I pressed pause. "Andréa came over today and told me what happened with Gabe's parents. It was bad, and Christine heard the whole thing." I recounted the whole story for Mike. Sadness crossed his face too.

He set his bowl of potato chips on the coffee table and handed me the baby. "Hang on a second. I'll be right back." When he returned a few minutes later, I made a questioning face. "I just wanted to give her one more kiss goodnight," he replied. "She pushes us away so much, sometimes I forget where all of her hurt comes from."

I knew exactly what he was talking about. Christine experienced a lot of uncertainty in her early life. It took its toll on her in so many ways, especially her ability to trust that the adults in her life would care for her and always be there for her. We turned our show back on, and the rest of the night was peaceful.

The next few days brought a little more stability to our newest addition. One week after Gabe arrived, I received a call from his caseworker. He had never been given any vaccinations and would need to catch up. I had been down this road before with two other children. I looked at my task list for the day and silently kissed any

amount of productivity goodbye. After checking the calendar, I realized that the health department had their shot clinic that day. I was
both relieved and disappointed. If I was going to get his shots, I
would need to leave the house immediately to get in line. I did just
that and thanked the Lord that Gabe was an easygoing baby.

Our county's health department was in the basement of the gov-
ernment building. I glanced at my watch and noted that we would
be there just as the doors opened. After going through the metal
detector twice, I made it to the elevator doors just in time for them
to close. I sighed. Trying not to be grouchy and failing, I waited for
the next elevator. When the doors opened again, I entered with at
least five other mothers, each toting one or two kids. I remembered
the days when my kids were younger and found myself grateful that
I wasn't trying to wrangle three small children, only one.

The line outside of the door to the shot clinic wrapped around
the hallway and through another set of double doors. I took my
place at the back and wished desperately that I had brought a book
to read. Over the course of the next hour, I watched inmates enter
through the guarded basement entrance as they were brought in
handcuffs and shackles to appear in court. I wondered about the
planning that must have been neglected to create an overlap of crim-
inals, mothers, and children. Gabe started crying about 30 minutes
into the wait. I bounced on my heels, swayed, propped the bottle
under my chin, and paced as far as I could without losing my place
in line.

The lady in front of me turned around and offered her help.
"Would you like me to give it a try?" she said with a smile. Her
daughter smiled at Gabe and nodded. Normally I would have been
offended or too proud to accept help, but something inside of me
was changing. This openness to others had caused me to realize once

again that I needed to be open to the kindness of those around me just as much as I needed to be open to sharing kindness.

I handed Gabe to the lady and introduced myself. "Hi, I'm Kristin, and this is Gabe."

She smiled and said, "I'm Maria, and this is Vita." She gestured to her daughter. Vita was eyeing the books I carried in the diaper bag. I asked her mom if it would be okay for her to look at one. Her mom agreed and for a few moments, we switched kids. Vita was delightful. I learned that she was four years old and that she already knew a lot of sight words. She was practically reading the book alone. Gabe calmed as Maria slowly swayed back and forth with him. I was grateful. The next hour flew by, and when we reached our turn at the clinic, I thanked Maria and waved goodbye to Vita.

The air inside the clinic was stuffy and warm. The dingy green walls and starburst countertops were leftovers from a previous generation. I found a seat between two very large women and waited for Gabe's number to be called. The women were not friendly, and I found myself longing to be back in the hallway reading books with Vita.

After another 45 minutes, Gabe's number was called. I took him to a back hallway, where the nurse weighed and measured him. She placed the paper measuring tape around his skull and made a comment of approval. "Well now, he's growing into a nice young man, isn't he?" She was a sweet older woman. I wondered if she had grandchildren. I imagined that she used that voice with them every time they brought her coloring pages filled with scribbles. Gabe smiled at her, and I immediately felt bad that she would have to give him his shots and ruin the sweet moment. Sensing my tension, she replied, "I'm very good at this. I know it hurts, but it will be over so fast, you won't even know it."

She proceeded to line up four brightly colored Band-Aids on her tray and double-checked her chart to make sure she was giving Gabe the right vaccinations. I had him in just a diaper and held him on my lap facing her. She gave all four shots faster than I could blink. Gabe squeezed a tear just as the nurse made a silly face at him and soothed him once again with her tone. I was truly amazed and told her so. Her peacefulness was a gift that I hoped never went unrecognized in a dreary place such as this.

Gabe took a little pain reliever as I buckled him into his seat, and he slept the rest of the way home. I treated myself to a soda, a treat I'd given up the week before, reasoning that I deserved just this one. It was worth every ounce of guilt I felt. We had time to run to the pharmacy on our way home, so at least the day didn't feel like a complete loss. I was glad to take care of Gabe, but it was hard to ignore that other things were falling through the cracks once again.

When the big kids got off the bus, they immediately wanted to know what was for dinner. Aaron was especially fixated on the menu. It sometimes frustrated me how much he obsessed about mealtime, but I reminded myself that he was hungry as a baby, and that was not a feeling that went away without years of security and trust. I sighed and felt a little sorry for myself that my day had gone on without any break. Aaron was frustrated with me because I didn't have a quick answer. He immediately went to the kitchen, and in the time it took me to change Gabe's diaper, I smelled something burning.

Aaron had poured oil into a pan and turned it on high. He was in the process of pouring a jar of pickles onto a plate of flour.

"Oh no!" I gasped. "What are you doing?" I yelled in shock. That was not the right move.

Aaron dropped to the floor and started to growl at me. I put the baby in his swing quickly, asking Grace to buckle him. Then I returned quickly to the kitchen to try to fix the situation. I turned the stove off and began to clean up the mess. I didn't say anything to Aaron but muttered under my breath about my disappointment and anger and frustration. Aaron was still crouched on the floor when I turned around to look at him. "Can we please not do this today, Aaron? Please?" I pleaded with a tone of sarcasm and exasperation.

He scrunched his fists up at me and unfurled himself. At his full height, he was still the size of a preschooler. His size was not intimidating, but his demeanor was. I snapped back to reality. Yes, I'd had a long day, but Aaron's brain was like a boiling pot every day. I knew better than to yell at him. I set the sponge down on the sink and crouched at eye level to him. "I'm sorry I yelled. We can't make fried pickles today. I need you to help me clean up, and then I would love to have you help me make dinner."

Grace turned the baby swing at an angle where she could keep one eye on Aaron while cooing at Gabe. It broke my heart to know how deeply all my children felt the tension that could erupt when one of their siblings felt dysregulated. Grace felt it the most but wouldn't talk about her feelings. I knew the stress was building up inside of her. Aaron calmed quickly and apologized for making the mess. He chose spaghetti for dinner, which was a favorite for everyone. Much to my relief, I found a package of frozen meatballs in the freezer. Spaghetti and meatballs could usually turn a grouchy day around for my kids faster than anything. Mike was working late, so the kids and I fixed an early dinner and had a little time to ride bikes before bedtime.

We ate dinner quickly and without much conversation. As we were clearing the table, Christine spoke up. "How long do you think Gabe is going to stay?"

I shrugged my shoulders in response. "I wish I knew. His case-worker is looking for family members to take him. She hasn't found anyone yet, but it's still early. Are you doing okay with him here?"

She nodded and paused for a moment before answering, "I like him a lot. I wish he could stay. I also know I would have liked a family member to come get me."

I didn't know how to answer her. Foster and adoptive children don't choose to lose their first families, and many struggle throughout life to find their identity. I knew that Christine longed to fit in somewhere and often felt that she didn't fit in with our family. It stung to hear her say the words out loud, but I was equally relieved she was talking about her feelings.

"I know. I'm sad that didn't happen for you too. I know you really would like to know your relatives." I resisted the urge to say more. So often, I wanted to take away her sadness, but that just isn't possible. We finished cleaning up in silence and went to the garage to gather bikes and the stroller.

Gabe was happy to be outside. He sat up and looked around while we walked. Aaron rode his bike like a stunt man with absolutely no concern for his own safety. Grace and Christine found a friend to play with about five houses away. I let them stay and told them I would be back to pick them up in a few minutes. As we rounded the corner of our block, a neighbor flagged me down and asked if she could walk with me. I nodded, surprised that she wanted to spend time with me. We talked for a bit, and then she got to the point. "My husband and I have been talking about foster care. I really want to become a foster parent, but I'm kind of worried," she admitted.

I didn't know where to begin. "Well, can I answer any questions for you?"

We spent the next half hour talking about what to expect as a foster parent. I was braced for the usual insensitive questions, but they never came. She had done her research and was well versed in adoption language. As we rounded the final corner of our block, I had my girls in my sight and waved. My neighbor began to wrap up the conversation as we neared the girls, but then she blurted out, "I was adopted."

I stopped. "I didn't know that! Is that why you are interested in foster care?"

She nodded, and we agreed to talk some more the following day.

I gathered my kids and returned home for bath time. The big kids were able to bathe on their own, but Aaron still liked me to pour bubbles into the tub in abundance. Gabe sat in his bouncy seat while I filled the tub, and Aaron talked incessantly about all the things he did that day and all the things he would like to do on all the days from that day until forever. I got a little lost in thought. I was thinking about the neighbor and the conversation we had. Often, I wanted to shut others out of our lives for fear that they might not be good for our family. I had almost brushed her off earlier, but I was so glad I hadn't. Keeping the doors open meant so much more than just foster care. It meant children, birth families, new friends, and even support for our own family that we hadn't yet realized we would need for ourselves. Keeping our doors open had already grown and stretched us in ways we hadn't anticipated.

12

NO GOODBYE

I was able to fit Gabe into some of Jonathan's old clothes, but we were running low on diapers, wipes, and items for the quickly approaching fall weather. I called Gabe's caseworker to see if we could get his clothing allowance. Each child coming into care should have a small amount of money to get them through the first few weeks. We knew that it should have arrived in the first 48 hours, but caseworkers were often juggling large caseloads, and the clothing allowance commonly fell through the cracks. The vouchers were typically in the form of gift cards to a store that was located about 40 minutes from my house. I was okay with that because the need for Gabe to have some long-sleeve shirts was increasing by the day.

His caseworker didn't answer the phone when I called with the inquiry. I left a message and decided to email as well. A few more days went by with no communication. While the kids were in school one day, I took Gabe to the store and bought enough basics to get us by for a little while.

I'm frugal when it comes to most things, but the baby section at any store is such a challenge for me. The tiny items are just too cute for words. I selected small blue socks, soft wraparound onesies with tiny snaps along the side, and a couple sleepers, one with an alligator across the chest and another with teddy bear ears sticking out of the top of the feet. I limited myself to one box of diapers, one box of wipes, and one can of formula, reminding myself that the per diem would be available soon and I could get him more items later. I resisted the cute blue baby bottles but could not resist the pale-green blanket with the satin edges. Pleased with my purchases, I checked out and groaned at the cost, which even after shopping the clearance, was more than I had intended to spend. Gabe was quiet during the whole trip, waking only once to take a bottle.

I checked again about the clothing allowance the following day, leaving a message for the caseworker to let her know that I had already purchased some clothes. I was not concerned about receiving the money back, just hoping for a way to get him a few more things. She did not return my call. I gave up trying to get Gabe's clothing allowance. His per diem would come at the end of the month anyway, and I had learned to stretch a dollar. The per diem for a child his age with no special needs was barely enough to cover the cost of formula and diapers. Our family had the resources to foster without much concern for money, but I often wondered how other families were able to provide for their foster children while working full-time jobs, paying for day care, and juggling the parental visitation schedules, appointments with specialists, and caseworker drop-ins.

After four weeks, our caseworker had still had no success with finding a relative to place Gabe with, so we began to settle in. Each day, Aaron ran to find Gabe as soon as he woke in the morning. He peeked over the edge of the baby's crib with a wide grin, raising his hands to his face and softly whispering, "Peekaboo, peekaboo, little baby. I see you." Even if Aaron woke him, I could never be angry. My heart melted seeing my little boy so completely in love with this baby. Grace, ever the caregiver, fixed a bottle each morning before making her own slice of toast with honey. She loved to cradle him in one arm while silently chewing and sipping a cup of herbal tea, just like a little adult. Christine often had a hard time trusting the adults in her life, but she cared for those smaller than her with great diligence. We were all wrapped around this baby's tiny little finger.

One morning, I waved goodbye to my children at the bus stop and returned home to complete my daily routine. Gabe and I went to the basement and gathered clothes from the bottom of the clothes chute. The laundry room was one of my favorite features in the house. It had a carpeted floor, shelves for supplies, a large counter where we could keep a basket for each person, and two washers and dryers. I enjoy doing laundry, which is a blessing because there has never been a shortage of this chore in our home.

I pulled the first load of clean laundry from the dryer and placed armfuls of fluffy warm towels into the first basket, creating a small nest in the center. I placed Gabe in the nest, and he smiled. I moved the basket to the other side of the laundry room and proceeded to switch the rest of the laundry over. I talked and sang to Gabe while I folded a few days' worth of tiny baby clothes, big kid PJs, and enough sheets and towels to fill a hotel. I reminded myself to check in with the kids about the appropriate number of towels per bath. I finished after a substantial amount of time and felt quite accomplished. Feeling like I could take on any task, I scooped Gabe up under one arm and a basket of clean blankets in the other.

When I reached the kitchen, I realized I had left my phone there. I glanced at it to see that I had three missed calls, all from the Department of Child Services. My heart sank. I listened to the message.

"Hello, Mrs. Berry. This is Ms. Hopkins. I am the new case manager assigned to Matthew's case. I need you to call me back as soon as possible."

I set the basket down and clung to Gabe while I dialed with

shaking hands. She picked up on the second ring. "Mrs. Berry, I'm glad you were able to get back to me." I sensed her agitation. "Matthew's aunt has been located. You will need to bring the baby to her this afternoon."

Without thinking, I responded, "He goes by Gabe."

Ms. Hopkins was not one to enjoy being corrected. "I'm sorry, what did you say?"

My voice was firmer. "He goes by Gabe, and my kids love him. They need to say goodbye." Ms. Hopkins was not in an accommodating mood. "He is not yours, Mrs. Berry. You will need to bring him to the office today by one." I cursed myself for not playing nice.

I gathered his things in a fog. I sent Mike a text simply stating that I was taking Gabe to his aunt. No explanation and no emotion. With complete numbness, I buckled Gabe into the car and drove him to DCS. I parked the car at the back of the busy parking lot and walked slowly toward the door. I stepped in a puddle and didn't register the feeling of cool moisture against my skin until I heard the squishing sound as I entered the large glass doors. I looked down at my right foot and noticed with detachment that my favorite pair of red ballet flats were ruined.

I stated my name at the front desk, asked for Ms. Hopkins, and then went to wait on the plastic couch. I scanned the room to see if I might recognize the aunt. I didn't. Mechanically, I fixed a bottle and fed Gabe while I waited. After 40 minutes, Ms. Hopkins revealed herself. She walked toward the couch and said curtly, "Is this all he has?" She gestured to the two duffel bags sitting next to my feet. I nodded that it was. She took the baby and began to grab the car seat.

I snapped to attention. "I can't give you that—it's mine."

"His aunt doesn't have a car seat," she grumbled in response.

By then, I was indignant, my fog lifting and the sadness

threatening to burst forth. "I paid for that. As a matter of fact, I paid for everything he has. I did not get the per diem or the clothing vouchers. I bought these things for him because he needed them. I was there for him. I was there." I gestured with a finger toward my own chest and gulped back a sob.

"This really is unnecessary, Mrs. Berry. You may say goodbye now." Her tone softened but only a little. I kissed Gabe on the forehead and whispered a nearly silent prayer into his tiny ear. I watched as Ms. Hopkins handed the baby to a disinterested-looking woman. I watched long enough to see that she did not smile or coo. She took him in her arms as if he was a burden. My heart nearly broke, and I turned and walked away.

My arms physically ached as I returned to the car. Without thinking, I stepped directly into the puddle with my left shoe this time. "Figures," I said to no one. I absently drove home while the empty car seat mocked me. Waves of grief ripped me from my shock. With each new wave came a new realization. He was not there. I would never see him again. He may not be in a good home. Then the worst realization yet—Christine, Grace, and Aaron. I pictured their tiny, hopeful faces, and the weight of it crushed me. When I pulled into the driveway, I pressed my forehead to the steering wheel and sobbed. When I finally freed myself from the seat belt, I looked up to see Mike rocking on one of the matching wooden rockers that he and the kids purchased for Mother's Day the previous year. He was waiting patiently for me. I'm not the affectionate one in our relationship, but on this day, I fell into his open arms and sobbed. When I was finally done, we walked inside and waited for the kids to come home.

The bus pulled into the neighborhood with an unmistakable screech. I had showered and splashed my face with cool water. Mike and I met the kids at the door. I knew that they sensed the shift because the bubbly play-bickering stopped as soon as they looked at us.

Christine spoke first. "What?" was all she said.

We each hugged them, and I said, "I have some news that is going to make you feel sad." Thankfully, Mike took over. "Remember that when we are fostering children, they have other families. Gabe has another family, and his aunt came to take him to live with her today."

Christine folded her arms and glared at us.

Grace said, "Oh, that's nice for Gabe."

Aaron kicked at the bottom rung of the banister until it gave way.

I was able to finish the conversation. "I know you are all feeling sad. Daddy and I are feeling sad too. Gabe is safe, and he is going to be in a good place until his mom and dad are able to live with him again." I didn't know if this was true, but I hoped that it was. The kids dispersed, and the rest of the night was spent in an eerie silence. Mike and I barely talked as well. We ate boxed macaroni and cheese for dinner, and I did not even force the veggies.

The next morning, I saw Aaron walk toward Gabe's crib and then turn abruptly. Grace stood in the kitchen next to the rack of drying bottles for a moment before pouring a bowl of cereal. Christine didn't say another word about Gabe. The morning felt tilted and uncertain. I drove the kids to school, not wanting to let them go quite yet. Mike was already at work. They kissed me goodbye and turned toward school and their friends.

The pit in my stomach grew as I turned out of the parking lot toward home. I didn't want to go there. When I was working outside of the home, I had loved my job. When I was staying home with my preschoolers, I had loved that job. But on that day, I felt as if I was the least-needed person on the planet. No children, no job. I drove around for a while until my phone pinged, notifying me of a text message. It was Nicole and Megan. They heard what happened and wondered if I had a little time for coffee. My first instinct was to continue wallowing, but the prospect of coffee was enticing. I clicked the turn signal and drove toward our favorite coffee shop.

I ordered a cup of vanilla hazelnut and wrapped my hands around the warm mug. The chilly morning caught everyone by surprise. After the harsh summer, the crisp air felt invigorating. I took a tentative sip to test the temperature and felt the hot liquid warm me. I shivered involuntarily and thought about Gabe. I wondered if he was warm. I imagined his aunt stopping to buy him a tiny jacket. My throat clenched, and I put the coffee mug down, no longer able to swallow. My friends showed up shortly after, and for a while, I forgot the feeling of anxious uncertainty. My cell phone sat silent on the table next to me, and I realized for the first time that I was not interested in keeping my doors open for a while.

My friends and I talked for an hour, and I was feeling much better. The phone buzzed and jumped across the table, surprising me. Noting the school's number on the screen, I answered quickly. "Mrs. Berry, this is Mrs. Schultz at the elementary school. I have Grace here in my office. She ran out of the classroom crying, and the teacher couldn't calm her. I found her under a table in the hallway. She did eventually come out, but she will not tell me what's wrong."

I put my head in my hands. "Can I talk to her?"

Her principal handed her the phone. Grace's voice was so small, the sound of it filled my heart with sadness. "I don't know why I ran out of the classroom, Mommy. I'm sorry," she said in a whisper.

"That's okay," I replied. "Do you think you might be sad about Gabe?"

She didn't respond but when the principal got back on the line, she told me that Grace was nodding her head. "I'm going to come get her," I said while picking my keys up and rising from the table. My friends waved goodbye.

My coffee spilled a little on my hand as I unlocked the car. An angry red mark spread across my knuckle as I resisted the urge to let out a yelp. I carefully moved the cup to my left hand, balanced the phone between my ear and shoulder, and turned the key while I filled the principal in on the abrupt change in our home. I apologized for not telling her earlier. She said she understood and supported me in coming to the school to check on Grace. I was grateful.

The silence in the car pressed in around me. I began questioning myself and my choice to live the life we had chosen. I wondered if we had heard God clearly in our calling. Maybe we were wrong to put our children through this roller coaster. Maybe we were wrong to put ourselves through the constant whirlwind of emotions.

I arrived at the school before I was able to process the questions floating around in my mind. I walked quickly from the parking lot to the first set of glass doors and pressed the buzzer. I didn't even announce myself. The voice on the intercom said, "Come on in, Kristin." The office administrator always greeted me with a friendly smile and some piece of friendly chatter that typically amused me. On this day, she gave me a half smile and waved me on with a gesture toward the principal's office.

I could see Grace's swinging legs just past the partially open door. I knocked as I opened it. Grace sat with her elbows on her knees and her head in her hands. She turned her eyes upward toward me and whispered, "Sorry, Mommy." She was so much smaller than I remembered. Her striped tights, pink corduroy skirt, and yellow sparkly shirt hung loosely on her lanky frame. She picked that shirt out for the first day of school and insisted on wearing it at least once a week, if not more. I had to hand-wash it to keep the glitter from coming off, and I'd cursed myself for buying such a high-maintenance garment, but this new perspective of her grabbed my heart. I would buy her a thousand handwash-only shirts if it would take away just a bit of her pain.

I nodded at the principal and then dropped to my knees beside Grace. "You have nothing to be sorry for," I said. She wrapped her little arms around me and cried. After a few moments, I looked at her face again. Her eyes were downcast, and her eyebrows wrinkled. "Look at my eyes, Grace. I'm not mad, and neither is Mrs. Schultz. It's okay to be sad. It's not okay to run out of the classroom. Next time you feel this way, please tell an adult, and we will try to help. Okay?"

She nodded in response.

"Would you like to get some lunch with me today?" I asked.

She looked surprised. "Really?"

I smiled. "Yes, let's go. We have a little time before you have to be back in class."

Grace and I ate a quick fast-food lunch before returning to school. She smiled halfway through her vanilla milkshake, and I felt certain that we were all going to be okay. Gabe would be okay too. Grace and I agreed to stop and pray for Gabe anytime we felt sad about missing him. She returned to school in much better spirits, and I made a mental note to check on Aaron and Christine later that day.

13

EMBRACING
THE HARVEST

I crawled out of bed on the first day of October and I knew instantly that I would have to give in and turn the furnace on. Pulling my sweatshirt over my sleep shirt, I padded down the stairs to the thermostat. I turned the dial and clicked the switch from off to heat. Mike had left for work early that morning, and I was surprised that he hadn't noticed the temperature. Rubbing my hands together, I went to the kitchen and filled a mug with the still piping-hot coffee. I reminded myself to thank him for always brewing a pot, even on the days he had to leave early. I took a sip and let it warm my tongue. Then I listened to the silence. It was too quiet. Our old oil furnace always made a sputtering resistance to the first cold day. I heard nothing. I sighed and descended to the basement.

Priming the heater was not a new task for me, but for some reason, I felt irritated. I removed the front panel easily and placed it on the floor beside my foot. I reached inside and cut myself on the sharp edge. I cursed under my breath and heard Aaron's sweet voice in response.

"Mommy! That's gonna cost you a quarter."

I turned around and couldn't help but smile at my son. "I'm sorry, I messed up," I admitted. The furnace was up and running within moments, and I scooped Aaron into my arms and carried him up the stairs. "You're going to get too big for this soon!" I said in mock exhaustion. The truth was that Aaron was quite small for his age and light as a feather too. We sat at the kitchen table together. I fixed him a cup of warm milk with a tiny bit of coffee, and he sipped his drink quite pleased with himself at being so grown. The heater emitted a warm oil smell that I had grown to love. It filled me with a sense of expectation and thrill for the upcoming season.

Christine and Grace bounded down the stairs in matching Tinkerbell nightgowns. "It's cold!" they said in unison through chattering teeth. Each ran toward the decorative registers on either side of the dining room. The heat warmed their tiny legs and caused their nightgowns to billow out around them. When they were finally warm enough, they grabbed bowls and poured their own cereal. The bus was about to come barreling through the neighborhood and I realized I hadn't pulled out the jackets. I ran to the basement while the kids put their shoes on. In the storage room, I pushed past the bins of baby items not currently in use and found the one with warm clothes. I pulled out three jackets and ran up the stairs. Aaron grabbed his without hesitation and ran out the door. Grace frowned at hers but followed Aaron. Christine simply said no and put hers on the floor, grabbing her bag. I sighed, wondering how the teen years were going to go with those two angels. I shrugged my shoulders and closed the door behind them.

I changed into jeans and a soft sweatshirt, skipping my shower. I just wanted to get out for a walk before I had to be at the school for Aaron's IEP (individualized educational plan) review later that morning. The crisp air filled my lungs, and I reveled in it. The park near our house had endless hiking trails, and I was ready to explore.

I parked the car in the deserted parking lot and headed down a familiar path. The river, which was overflowing, soon covered the path. I gingerly stepped around it and climbed to higher ground. The woods were muddy, and my grimy old sneakers made sucking sounds as the mud refused to release them. I laughed out loud and realized that an onlooker might find my behavior disturbing. As I reached the top of the ravine, I turned to look back on my climb. Just then, the wind kicked up and a shower of orange and yellow leaves swirled around me.

I sat on a half-rotted stump and watched in silence. The creek tumbled over the river rock. The leaves fell softly. The wind whispered, and the chilly air hit my warm cheeks with a delightful, brisk alertness. I relished it all. I had not been able to pray since our last placement. I felt so unsure of our direction as a family. "I'm listening," I whispered. I don't know how long I sat there. The silence filled me and peace along with it. Finally, my alarm sounded on my phone, alerting me to head toward the school meeting. I still didn't know what our family was going to do, but I did know that God had not lost sight of me.

Aaron's IEP meeting was typical. He has FASD (fetal alcohol spectrum disorder), which makes it difficult for him to control his impulses. He struggles with reading, writing, and auditory processing and has many cognitive delays. However, to most, he looked like any other typically developing student. Requests for conferences, behavior plans, and classroom accommodations were often met with resistance. Well-meaning teachers often saw Aaron's ability to be articulate, funny, and kind to be an indication that his diagnosis was wrong. The meeting touched a little on this line of thinking, but as he had begun to age chronologically, his maturity had lagged behind his peers in more significant ways. His teacher and classroom aid expressed concerns that I wasn't prepared for. I was used to fighting for him to keep services in the classroom. This time, his teacher laid his evaluation in front of me. I began to leaf through the daunting stack of papers, and as I read, I became more concerned too. He was trailing behind his peers in every area. Even with accommodations, he had failed every state assessment for students his age.

Everyone at the meeting assured me that he would not be held back for not passing the standardized tests. We worked together to add extra one-on-one time during the day for him to relearn each subject outside of the classroom, after the typical whole-class instruction. He would be allowed to go to the resource room to visit with his special education teacher throughout the day to get a little sensory input on the trampoline or swing—his favorite. I nearly cried when the principal patted my hand and reminded me that her daughter received similar services. "Our kids are going to be okay," she said with an understanding smile. Gratitude overwhelmed me, and I grabbed a tissue to dab at my moist eyes.

I left the appointment and called Mike. I knew he was headed into a meeting and didn't have time to process my feelings with me. I told him quickly that the meeting went well and that we were going to have to push for more services with Aaron.

"I keep wishing this would just go away," he said.

"I know what you mean," I agreed. His words were so true for me too. In the back of my mind, I always believed that Aaron would catch up, that maybe there would be a time we would look back on all of this with disbelief. We knew that wasn't likely. There is no cure for FASD; we knew he would need some type of support throughout his life. I hung up and pulled into the driveway. I spent the afternoon catching up on the mountain of laundry that had accumulated in the hamper, then sorted through the cold weather clothes, finishing just in time for Aaron to burst through the door.

He wrapped his little arms around me and then pointed to his shirt, which boasted a "superstar" sticker.

"I got it for my spelling test, Mommy!" he shouted with pride, which nearly broke my heart in two. I hoped he would never lose that enthusiasm.

The entire month of October brought peace and reconnection for my family. We traveled to the pumpkin patch one sunny afternoon, where Mike met us on his way home from work. The fall colors were brilliant, and much to our surprise, storms held off for most of the fall, allowing the brilliant colors to remain. I remembered to prepare with galoshes, snacks, jackets, and most importantly, adorable matching fall outfits for the photographs I would surely take while there. We entered through the small country store and good smells surrounded us. Cinnamon, apple cider, and freshly baked pumpkin pies made our mouths water. Mike and I promised the kids we would choose one treat after getting our pumpkins. The kids squealed with anticipation and discussed what they would choose as they headed toward the bright-red wagons that would take us out to a field to choose pumpkins.

We climbed aboard and squeezed in to find a space among the multitude of families. We lined the kids up on either side of us to curb any potential bickering and prolong the fun we were already having. Grace sat next to Mike, then Aaron, then me and finally Christine. Mike took his camera and snapped a picture of the five of us. Tucking the camera in the front pocket of his jacket, he looked over Aaron's head at me and said, "I'm so glad to be here with my family." I nodded.

Just then Aaron's shoe flew off his foot and landed among the pumpkins and into the mud. I shook my head. Grace piped up, "Not again, Aaron!" That child was always losing his shoe. We grabbed the kids' hands and jumped off the wagon before the stop and began the search for the missing boot. "Thank goodness it's bright green," I thought. When the kids were much smaller, I always dressed them in bright colors—especially Aaron, who tended to get lost.

Mike found the missing shoe, and we all cheered. We spent the next 30 minutes walking toward the rest of the group and carefully choosing the best pumpkin for each of us. Grace and Christine always chose one that was round to the point of perfection. Aaron tended to pick the oddest-looking one he could find—usually one that wouldn't even stand on its own—and then we would laugh and laugh as he tried to carve it into something presentable.

This year was no exception. The girls lugged their pumpkins to the wagon while I carried Aaron's, and Aaron hitched a ride on Mike's shoulders. We climbed aboard the wagon in the same order we'd arrived in, but to my surprise, Christine crawled onto my lap. She hadn't done that since she was a toddler, and even then it was rare. She curled up, and as we began our ride, she whispered, "Juniper would have loved this." She continued, "It's hard when they leave, but I'm glad kids can come stay with us." She said nothing more on the subject, just slipped off my lap and grabbed her pumpkin.

We made it back to the little store in time to get the last three candied apples and a few cups of warm apple cider. After loading the pumpkins into the back of the car, we agreed that the girls would ride home with the girls and the boys with the boys. We all knew that it meant an unofficial race was underway. Mike gave me a thumbs-up while the girls shouted from the back seat, "Watch your back! You better watch your back!" Aaron's little voice could be heard from Mike's car: "Don't mess with us! You can't beat this." Then his laughter burst forth straight from his belly. "See you at home!" I shouted. I don't remember who won. I really don't, but since I'm the one writing this book, I'm going to say it was the girls who won that day.

Christine, my budding fashion designer, helped me make our Halloween costumes. We cut and glued and sewed and ripped seams and sewed again until we had five of the best costumes we had ever created. Mary Poppins and Bert, Venus and Serena Williams, and one very adorable vampire bat. Trick-or-treating approached, and we talked about nothing else. Mike and I worried too. Aaron had an aggressive reaction to food dyes and a lot of difficulty processing sugar. We bought alternatives to trade out when the kids got home. They were excited about the candy we bought and secretly hoped we didn't have any trick-or-treaters come to our door so they could keep the thousands of glow sticks we had purchased to hand out.

Each year, we threw a party for our neighbors and friends, and this year was no exception. We decided to invite Juniper and Jonathan's family too. They accepted our invitation, and as the day approached, we felt even more excited. We decorated our house with spiderwebs, pumpkin candles, and cardboard bats, hanging them from every possible light fixture. I chopped and sautéed until the entire house smelled like chili and corn bread. Mike built a fire in a portable firepit that we pulled onto the driveway so that the adults could sit there and pass out candy.

Guests arrived right on time and quickly dressed in their costumes. The big kids took off with their friends to gather candy around the neighborhood. Mike and I agreed to take turns with Aaron. He was not able to control himself when it came to candy, and if I'm being honest, I wasn't the best example of self-control either. June and Jonathan hadn't shown up yet when we started out, but as we rounded the corner of our neighborhood, I saw their van pull up. Aaron saw them too and shouted. He was excited to see the

kids. We ran to the van excitedly but realized right away that something was wrong. Juniper's costume was covered in vomit. "Oh no!"
I said, resisting the urge to parent her. Her mom stepped in and
wiped her down with some baby wipes. "I don't have anything else
for her to wear," she said in an ashamed tone. Now, that was a problem I could solve. "I think we can fix that!" I said. Aaron agreed
and led the way to a huge bin of costumes that my kids loved playing with. Juniper grabbed a soft furry tiger outfit I had forgotten
we owned. It was perfect. Aaron began to get agitated as June got
dressed, and I told her parents we would meet them outside. They
nodded.

Aaron and I trick-or-treated until we were exhausted. Meanwhile, our house was filling with guests who were hungry for some
chili. The crowd was bustling, and as I called everyone into the
kitchen to pray before dinner, I was filled with a sense of awe that we
were so lucky to have these friends. We dished out warm chili and
hot apple cider until every plate was full. Families gathered around
tables and spilled out to the driveway, where more people pulled
chairs close to the fire. We stayed up too late, and when our guests
left, we put the kids to bed with clean teeth and dirty faces. We
would bathe in the morning. We reasoned that it was a special night.

The following day, the kids didn't have school—a rarity. I was
relieved. They slept in, and I began the task of making phone calls.
It was something I dreaded. My first call was to the Department of
Child Services to inquire about our per diem for Gabe, which had
never come. I wondered if I might be able to get reimbursed for the
clothing as well. I knew it was a long shot, but I had kept the receipts
just in case.

After being transferred to three different people, I gave my information once again. The woman I spoke to asked me to spell Gabe's
full name over and over and then, with an air of decisiveness, told

me they had no record of a child by that name. I was shocked and pushed forward. Eventually, she changed her tone to frustration and told me she would transfer me to a supervisor. I felt blindsided. Was she accusing me of making this up? I waited on hold for 30 minutes and then the line disconnected. Grace and Christine were awake and fixing bowls of cereal. I slammed the phone down on the table and sighed in frustration. They both looked up with questioning eyes. "Oh, babies, I'm sorry. Just a frustrating phone call." They nodded, and I decided not to call back until I'd cooled off a bit.

We never did get the issue resolved. After hours of phone calls and frustrating conversations and unreturned emails, I dropped the issue, but I felt certain that I could no longer work with a county that would lose all documentation of a child like that. We held a dual license, allowing us to foster for two counties, and so Mike and I agreed that we would respond to the other county for now and take some time off from the organization we had been working with. Their attitude toward our family was demoralizing. We often felt unheard and criticized. We knew we needed a little space for a while. That magical fall, we ended with as much hope as we began with, but also a little more clarity on the reality of setting boundaries even while our doors were open. With the excitement of the holiday season approaching, we held our three children a little tighter and prayed for our hearts to be open to others again. We asked that we would have the wisdom to serve others while allowing ourselves to be helped in a way that was healthy for all of us.

14

ARE WE READY FOR TEENAGERS?

November began like a gentle breeze. We packed away our Halloween decorations and began to plan for a big Thanksgiving dinner with family. My sister was coming to town for the big day, and between the two families, we had three major food allergies to contend with. Dairy, peanuts, and eggs were taken off the menu, but we accepted the challenge and began exchanging recipes over text and email as the day approached. The kids practiced for their school program on gratitude, and the catchy songs became so deeply embedded into my subconscious that I believed I could be an understudy for even the most talented third grader. By the third week of November, the menu was finalized, including all meals and snacks for two families of five.

My sister began the six-hour drive with her three children in tow. Their family is also a multiracial, adoptive family. It was nice to know that when our children were together, they wouldn't have to explain or defend any part of their stories. There was always an unspoken, unashamed understanding between them. Snow started falling as soon as they left their little town in Wisconsin. Traffic was bad, and they called to say that six hours was looking more like eight. The girls generously agreed to loan their room to our relatives. They set up sleeping bags in our room and giggled with the anticipation of a sleepover with Mommy and Daddy. Christine and I made up their beds, and Grace wrote little notes welcoming them to leave on their pillows, since we knew the kids would be asleep by the time they arrived. They called again around Milwaukee to check in. The drive was okay, just slow going. My niece Luna, who was just a preschooler, had already been crying for two hours, and they were exhausted.

My phone rang a few hours later, and I assumed it was my sister without checking the screen. I held the phone to my ear while stirring the make-ahead mashed potatoes. "Hello?"

The voice on the other end was not my sister. "Hello, is this Kristin Berry?" an unfamiliar voice said.

"This is she."

"This is Frank Dallas from Fayette County Department of Child Services. I talked with your friend Megan tonight, and she said you might have an opening in your home for a teenager." I pressed the off switch on the handheld mixer so I could hear him clearly. He continued, "All our homes are full, and we are looking at families who have a dual-county license. I know it's a holiday. Are you able to take a 15-year-old?"

My mind raced. "Hang on a second, Frank, I'll be right back." I cupped my hand over the phone and went to find Mike. He was arranging a tangled mess of wires behind our new television. His priority was football. He looked up with a grin, quite pleased with himself.

I smiled and pointed to the phone. "It's Fayette County. Can we take a 15-year-old girl?"

He took a deep breath before replying. "What do you think?"

I shrugged my shoulders. "You know what shelter care is like. I can't imagine any child having to spend Thanksgiving in a shelter."

He nodded. I removed my hand from the phone and told Frank I could be at the office in 30 minutes. He thanked me.

I wiped up the mess from the mashed potatoes and secured plastic wrap over the casserole dish. After rearranging the stacks of Thanksgiving fare, I slipped the potatoes into the refrigerator, then shrugged my coat over my shoulders and grabbed my van keys.

Aaron saw me get my keys and ran to get his shoes. "I'm gonna go too, okay, Mommy?" I couldn't resist his cute face, and so I agreed.

He buckled himself into his booster seat while I explained where we were going. "Sometimes big kids need a home too, okay? I want us to be nice to this girl. She is going to be feeling sad about losing her family like this tonight."

Aaron nodded. "What is her name?"

I paused as I stuck the keys in the ignition. Had I forgotten to ask Frank the child's name? I started the car and answered, "I don't know. We'll have to ask her when we get there."

The drive was quick on the empty roads. We weaved through the streets of our small town until houses gave way to frozen cornfields. I loved the Midwest, but there was something about the brown upon brown upon more shades of brown that filled our state each winter that stung my eyes. Just as I was cursing the desolate, chilly view before me, the melting sun, which was dropping low, worked its magic. The sky turned pink and then red. Rays of gold touched the long-forgotten stumps of cornstalk that stood in rigid rows along the frosty fields. The silhouettes of barren trees looked black and flat across the landscape, as if an artist had drawn them there with coal. "Beautiful," I murmured.

Aaron whispered from the back seat, "Beautiful."

The trusty GPS chirped directions in a voice I found quite condescending. "Turn left in 100 feet. Turn left," the automated voice
commanded. I rolled my eyes, but I obeyed, and we pulled up in
front of the Department of Child Services office. I shifted the car
into park, and Aaron unbuckled despite my warning to stay put.
The office was dark, but I could see what I assumed was Frank's
hatchback parked under the single streetlamp. Frank got out of his
car and motioned for his passenger to do the same. To my surprise,
a lanky, sullen boy climbed out, unfolding his body and stretching before reaching into the back seat for a single duffel bag. He
walked around the car to stand beside Frank. I got a closer look as
he brushed his scraggly black hair out of his eyes.

"Oh, I thought you said a girl," I said before thinking.

Frank looked surprised. "Well, I didn't. This is Emmanuel. Is
that okay?" He hesitated as he finished the sentence.

I shook off my mistake with a quick nod of my head. "Oh, yes, of
course. I'm sorry, I was just surprised. It's nice to meet you, Emmanuel." I stuck my hand out to shake his. His grip was limp and non-
committal. He didn't make eye contact with me, but I followed his
gaze toward Aaron. I gestured to the small child. "This is Aaron."

Emmanuel bent down toward Aaron and looked at him through
his bangs. "Hey, kiddo, I'm Manny." Aaron high-fived him and
showed him to the car. I was grateful Aaron had talked his way into
accompanying me.

Manny slid his tattered blue duffel into the back seat and climbed
in next to Aaron, tucking his skateboard under his long legs. I could
see them in the rearview mirror and smiled at Aaron, who gave me
a thumbs-up. He talked Manny's ear off all the way home. "Hey,
Manny, do you have a skateboard? I have a skateboard. My mom
won't let me go to the skate park without a helmet. She says I can't

afford to lose any more brain cells!" At this, he burst into laughter and then continued. "I played football last year. It was supposed to be flag football, but I have a lot of aggression, and I forgot. I tackled someone. Someone tackled me too. Maybe some other kids are impulsive too. I don't know. I got a concussion. Have you ever had a concussion?" The kid did not take a breath the entire way home. I gave Manny an apologetic smile in the mirror, but he seemed grateful for the distraction Aaron was providing.

Mike and the girls had paused the Thanksgiving preparations while I was gone to disassemble the crib in the guest room and make the twin bed up with a pretty set of pink and purple polka dot sheets, topped with a sequined comforter from Christine's bed. Christine felt that if a kid could not be home on Thanksgiving, she should at least have something pretty in her bedroom. It was hastily thrown together, but Mike and the girls had stood back and admired the quick transformation of the new child's room.

The sound of the garage door opening alerted them to our arrival. They bounded down the stairs and rounded the corner to see the same surprise I had encountered only 40 minutes earlier.

Christine's confusion was evident. "What is this?" she questioned before I could explain.

"This is Manny," Aaron offered. "Mom made a mistake. Manny is a boy, not a girl!" He gestured to me and rolled his eyes for effect.

"Thanks, Aaron. Yes, that's true. I thought I was picking up a girl, but this is Manny. He's a boy. It would be nice for everyone to say hello."

Grace was always shy at first. "Hi," she whispered.

Christine looked him up and down one more time. "Do you need a haircut? Sometimes foster kids need a haircut, but a judge has to make an order in the court. Did you know that?"

Manny nodded. "Yes, I do know that. This isn't my first time in foster care. How about you?"

Christine looked him directly in the eye. "I'm not in foster care anymore. I was adopted."

Mike and I exchanged glances. This conversation was a little more intense than we had anticipated for the first meeting. Mike interjected, "All right, everyone, we have a big day tomorrow. Let's show Manny his room." I followed them up and almost laughed at the sight of it, outfitted for an eight-year-old princess.

Grace and Christine looked at Manny before going to brush their teeth. "You can keep our stuff in here for tonight, and then maybe Mom and Dad will get you something you like for your room."

He laughed and graciously said, "I like it. Thanks."

Mike and I tucked the kids into bed and kissed them, thanking them for their patience and flexibility. They showed hospitality, and we were proud of them for that. The girls were settled into our room for their special sleepover. They were excited about everything, and the bedtime routine took a lot longer than usual. They needed to have every question answered immediately. Some were about Manny, and some were about the relatives who were on their way. Some were just plain silly. When the routine finally turned to stalling, we kissed them and closed the door. I opened it a crack and whispered one more thing. "Don't you dare get in my bed and drool all over my special pillow!"

They burst into another fit of laughter and responded in unison, "We won't, Mommy, we swear!" I was 100 percent certain that they would be in my bed when I returned. I was right.

Once lights were out, we knocked on Manny's door. "Can we show you around?" Mike asked. Manny agreed. The three of us crept down the carpeted stairs, hoping to encourage the younger three to stay in their beds. We showed Manny where to find the dishes, food, pantry, bathroom, soap, and extra toilet paper and then asked if we forgot anything. It was obviously awkward for all of us.

"We're going to finish making Thanksgiving dinner. Do you want to come down and watch TV or something?" He didn't want to hang out with us but agreed anyway. Mike finished straightening up the house while I filled one Crock-Pot with allergen-free green-bean casserole and another with sweet potatoes. I attempted a few conversations.

"So what school do you go to?"

His almost-one-word answers stopped me before I could get started. "Emerson High."

Second attempt: "Oh, that's cool. We know a lot of kids who go there. Do you know Emily Smith?" He shook his head. "Do you know Paul Barger?" Again, he shook his head.

Mike piped up from the other room. "Hailee Fitzgerald?" Once again, he shook his head. I gave up for a bit and let the silence sit.

Mike came into the kitchen as I finished preparing the turkey. I disinfected the counter and scrubbed the sink while Mike tied the corners of a very full trash bag. "Anyone want some hot chocolate?" I offered. Mike nodded, and Manny perked up a little. I put a couple of cookies on a plate and some veggies on another and then set three hot cups of cocoa on the table and topped them with marshmallows. The three of us sat down.

I started first. "Manny, I know this is awkward. It is for us too. I don't know what brought you here, and you do not have to tell us anything. We want you to feel as comfortable as you can. Okay?" He nodded. I warmed my hands on the mug.

Mike continued. "This is kind of a crazy weekend to be here; I'm sorry about that. Our family is coming in town tonight, so when you wake up, there will be three more kids here! It's going to be a little nuts."

Manny nodded again and asked, "Were all of your kids in foster care?"

Mike responded, "No, just Aaron and Christine. You said you've been in foster care before?"

He nodded once then opened his mouth and closed it again. "This is the fifth time. My mom got arrested tonight. Frank picked me up at the police station. I hate that place." Manny picked with one long fingernail at a splatter of paint left there from a long-ago craft project. Mike and I stayed silent just in case Manny wanted to say more. To our surprise, he continued, "She'll get out. She always does. I just have to stick it out for a little bit. They took my sister too this time. She and my mom got in a fight with someone in the Dollar Store parking lot. I hate when they do that. She's in detention."

I raised my eyebrows and tried not to look shocked. "How old is your sister?"

"Thirteen." With that, the conversation about foster care was over. We didn't push him further.

The subject shifted to Manny's love of skateboarding. Neither of us had anything to add, so we just listened. Manny was very proud of every scar and broken bone he had earned while skating. It was impossible not to like the kid. He pointed to a nasty scar reaching from his wrist to his elbow. "I ran through a sliding glass door! I could have died. My sister and I were playing chase in the house." He laughed at the memory, but I felt a little sick to my stomach at the sight of the jagged, wrinkled skin. Pointing to a mark just beneath his bangs: "Fell out of a tree." Another on his foot: "Skateboarding. You should have seen that one, seriously. I have the video. I'll show it to you guys tomorrow. It was sick." I tried not to pass out. Mike handles blood less well than I do, and I thought I might have to pick him up off the floor. Manny nearly fell off his chair with laughter when he saw our faces. Pushing his chair away from the table, he excused himself and headed for bed.

Realizing how late it was, I called my sister to see if she and the kids were close by. They were less than an hour away. My sister sounded exhausted. I could hear my niece in the background whimpering. "Oh no, is that Luna?"

She replied flatly, "Mm-hmm."

I felt terrible for my three-year-old niece, my sister, and for that matter, everyone in the car who had been listening to the meltdown for seven hours. Transition can be so tough, something I knew it firsthand from my own children. I promised my sister and brother-in-law a pot of strong coffee the next morning. They both thanked me and returned to their drive.

Mike retired. He's a morning person, and the night had already worn on long past his typical bedtime. I pulled a book from the shelf and settled into my favorite chair, then flicked the reading lamp on and sat beneath the warm glow. Around 11:00 p.m., I heard the car pull into the driveway. I folded the blanket onto the back of the chair and dog-eared the corner of the page. I pulled my boots on and ran out front to help them bring their stuff in. Expecting to see my nieces and nephews sound asleep, I quietly opened the sliding door on the side of the van. They were not asleep. The look on my sister's face told the story. I shook my head in understanding and offered to carry my youngest niece inside. Unbuckling her car seat, I scooped her into my arms. "I don't like the car, Aunt Kristin," she murmured.

"I know, I know," I soothed. She buried her head in my shoulder. My sister and brother-in-law grabbed the other two and all the stuff they could carry. We shuffled up the stairs to the girls' room—the largest in the house—and dropped their things there. I placed Luna on her bed and pulled the blankets up around her. Then I turned to Everett, who was six, and Honey, who was about to turn eight. I kissed each one of them on the forehead and told them how happy I was to have them there. They smiled and rolled over on their cots, content to finally sleep.

My sister, her husband, and I crept back out to the car and unloaded the rest of their luggage. We met back up in the kitchen, and I brought out round two of the midnight snacks. I sat chips and dip in the center of the table and filled water glasses for each of us. The warm glow of the kitchen light felt cozy despite the frazzled emotions that already belonged to this day. We sat around the table a little longer, and when the clock ticked 12:01, we all agreed that this would be a new day. As we swept crumbs into the trash and dropped cups into the sink, I remembered to tell them we had a guest—a new foster son. They were surprised, but no one had the energy to talk more.

Just as I pulled my fuzzy pajama top over my head, I heard my niece begin to cry. She loved being at our house and loved her cousins, but often even a small change could trigger her memories of the time she spent in foster care. I knew that this night was going to be difficult. I slipped my socks on and crept down the hallway to knock on the door. My sister opened it a crack and peeked out.

"I know this was a rough day today. Would it be okay for me to take Luna to the family room with me to relax so you can get some sleep?"

My sister simply said thank you and opened the door for me to come inside. I lifted Luna from her bed and whispered, "You are having a really rough day. Mommy said it would be okay for us to read a book on the couch. What do you think?" She nodded. We shuffled downstairs, and I grabbed a few of my favorites off the overstuffed bookshelf.

First, we read a book called *Sisters*, which my mom always told me was written for me and my sister. That wasn't true, but I loved it anyway. Then we read *A Snowy Day*. Luna put her thumb in her mouth and smiled at the picture of Peter making prints in the snow. By the time I read the last page, she was asleep. I pulled a throw around her and reached for the corner of a blanket that was dropped over the back of the couch. It was just out of reach, the velvety fabric slipping through my fingers each time I pulled. Finally, the blanket shifted enough to fall into my grasp. I wrapped it around my legs, put my head back, and allowed my eyes to fall closed.

15

CRAZY HOUSE, FULL HEART

On Thanksgiving morning, I woke with a start to the sound of Christine descending the stairs. At first, I thought she had fallen but soon realized it was just her typical heavy-footed enthusiasm. Luna's tiny legs were trapped over mine and her head was resting on a couch cushion. My neck was stiff, and I turned my head from side to side while rubbing the muscles.

Luna unfolded herself slowly and rubbed her eyes. She looked around with confusion and then smiled. "Auntie, it's Thanksgiving!" she shouted. She took off after her cousin, who was already pouring a bowl of cereal. Within minutes, the house was alive with people. Mike, always the early riser, had brewed a pot of coffee, and the aroma hit my nose just as I hugged each child good morning. I poured a cup for myself, and my sister entered the kitchen looking much less frazzled.

"Thank you! Did she stay up all night? I'm so sorry."

I shook my head no. "She slept through, and it only took two books. I think she really wore herself out in the car last night." I glanced at the clock and realized I should have put the turkey in the oven two hours earlier. I did a quick calculation and decided we were having Thanksgiving dinner instead of Thanksgiving lunch. No harm done. Rebecca agreed, and I was thankful to have such flexible family.

Manny appeared in the kitchen wearing a pair of dorm pants, a wrinkled T-shirt, and socks with a hole in the toe. Aaron jumped to attention, taking responsibility for introductions. "Everyone, this is Manny. He's my new brother. Well, for now at least."

With his eyes cast downward and a crooked smile in place, he greeted everyone. The kid looked lost in the crowd, so Mike quickly rescued him, showing him the breakfast options.

Aaron took charge again. "I'm having Rice Krispies, but you can have Cheerios. Wait, do you want Rice Krispies? I'll get you that instead." Aaron poured the cereal into two bowls. He tipped the jug of milk over the first bowl using both hands. It poured over the sides of the bowl and onto the counter. He shrugged and moved to the second bowl before I could reach him to grab the gallon jug.

"Aaron!" I shouted.

Aaron surveyed the mess and then shrugged his shoulders, handing the larger bowl to Manny. He went to the cabinet and grabbed a towel. He did a mediocre job of cleaning up, doing more smearing than sopping. Still, I was proud of how he was handling the situation.

Mike leaned out of earshot of Aaron and whispered to Manny, "You don't have to eat that if you don't want to." Manny reached into the bowl, took a big bite, and then smiled at Mike and Aaron. "Yum."

Mike mouthed the words "thank you." Manny just nodded. I cleaned up the rest of the mess while Aaron showed Manny the dining room and grabbed his cousin Everett along the way, announcing,

"The boys are going to sit in the dining room. The girls can sit in the kitchen."

I shook my head. "Aaron, please don't leave your sisters out," I said with a warning.

Grace piped up, "We don't want to sit with them anyway. Right, Christine, Honey, Luna?" They all nodded and made their way to the kitchen table.

I was grateful to have made the food the night before. We didn't have much work to do, which left plenty of time to spend together. Rebecca brought a ton of crafts with her, so we cleared the kitchen table to make way for the kids to create. Rebecca retrieved the crafts from her suitcase and I dug through the cabinet looking for some glue sticks. I found glitter, three pairs of scissors I thought were missing, tissue paper, and two jars of dried-up paste. Finally, I found an unopened glue stick. In a house with little kids, that was like finding gold. I held it up like a prize and Grace began to giggle. When the boys saw the craft supplies spread out on the table, they decided they weren't too cool for the girls after all. Aaron and Everett pulled chairs up next to their sisters, and Manny excused himself to get changed. Rebecca and I got the turkey in the oven and began heating casseroles and plugging in Crock-Pots. Before long, the kitchen smelled amazing.

Craft time lasted much longer than expected, and dinner preparations were well on their way when the kids finally lost interest. The kitchen floor looked like the site of a natural disaster, but everyone was happy. It was a small price to pay. My brother-in-law, Derek, and Mike were ready for their annual game of backyard football. We started the tradition with all my brothers and sisters years ago, but this game would be significantly less aggressive, since the oldest child wasn't yet ten. At least, I hoped the two grown men would remember how little the kids were.

The weather was beautiful but a little chilly. Rebecca and I insisted the kids wear coats, hats, gloves, and boots. They rolled their eyes at us but complied. Just as they were about to head outside, Manny came into the kitchen. He grabbed a coat and his cruddy pair of tennis shoes and followed everyone outside. Rebecca and I seized our chance for some peace and quiet. We cleared the table once more and cursed the inventor of glitter. I brewed another pot of coffee. The timer went off on the pot, and I grabbed two large mugs from the cabinet above the coffee maker. We settled in at the table, which provided an excellent view of the touch football game taking place just outside the large kitchen window.

"Things have been hard this year with Luna," she started. I nodded, waiting for her to continue. "Her biological family is everywhere in our town. Most of them are nice, but I can see that it triggers Luna to see them at the grocery store, the day care center, the park. They are happy to see each other, but when we get home, I know she is going to have nightmares again. That's the hardest thing. The family that loves her aren't the people who hurt her, but I think it just reminds her of how things used to be." She trailed off and I wanted to ask more, but just then, a stream of kids burst through the back door, looking for a snack. My sister and I exchanged a quick glance to say we would pick this conversation up later.

I wondered out loud how we were going to afford the teenage years if the kids kept up all this eating. Aaron reminded me loudly, "We are growing! It's our job to grow, Mama. Don't stop feeding us!" He theatrically dropped to the floor in mock starvation. I patted his head and promised I would keep feeding his growing body with only one request—that he support me in my old age using his lucrative career as an actor. He nodded and smiled.

They didn't stay inside for long; the day was just too beautiful to spend it inside. We all agreed to head to the park while the turkey finished cooking. A small park with a playground was just a block from the house so we decided to walk. The air had warmed since breakfast, and soon we all removed our jackets to soak up what we knew would be one of the last warm days before the harsh Midwest winter really set in. Manny awkwardly asked if he could stay back. He had been through so much, and the poor kid just looked like he needed a break. Nothing in my body felt nervous about leaving him in the house. I checked with Mike to see what he thought, and he agreed, so we both said yes.

Christine could spin and swing all day—it made me dizzy just to look at her. Grace, on the other hand, still braced herself as she climbed the play set. She gingerly crept up the tall ladder at a snail's pace. Once she reached the slide, she gripped the edges and slowed her pace as she made her way to the bottom. Christine was hanging upside down on the monkey bars and called to her younger sister to try it. Grace simply said, "No thanks," and went back to repeatedly climbing the tall ladder and then inching her way down the slide.

Aaron yelled from across the playground, "I'll try it!" He was on top of the monkey bars in a flash. Instead of wrapping his legs around the bars, he began to balance himself on top like a tightrope. My heart nearly stopped. I saw Mike move toward him slowly so as not to startle him.

"Please be careful, Aaron," I pleaded. He ignored both of us and kept going. Fearless. I couldn't breathe. Then he slipped, teetered, and then caught himself. Not wanting to give in to the cautions of the adults, he made a silly face and then swung his legs over the bar, gripping the one parallel to it with his hands, and swung himself free. His little feet dangled about three feet off the ground. He jumped down without hesitation, rolled in the mulch, and then laughed, completely pleased with himself.

I finally breathed. Rebecca said, "Looks like you should get him into gymnastics." I just rolled my eyes and called the kids to begin the short walk home. The alarm on my phone went off just then to remind me to check the turkey. The kids reluctantly agreed to leave.

When we arrived home, the cozy, warm scents of the holiday greeted us. Mike and Derek took the kids to get washed and changed for dinner while Rebecca and I placed the piping hot food on the table. The doorbell rang, and I jumped. I had completely forgotten that Christine and Aaron's birth family were supposed to join us for dessert. I hit my forehead with an oven mitt. How could I have let that slip my mind? I answered the door to see the kids' first mom and grandma standing there.

"So here's the deal, we got really behind on dinner. I hope you guys are hungry!" Grandma shook her head at me but accepted the offer, and Rebecca grabbed two more dinner plates. Manny had materialized by then and offered to get two more chairs. I made the introductions quickly as I hugged the kids' birth mom. She and I were friends long before the kids came to live with us. There were years of healing between us, and every time we got together, it was a step toward healing for the kids as well. Aaron and Christine raced down the stairs at the sound of their voices.

Grace looked a little lost. They were always kind to her, but I could tell that her lack of relationship with her biological family was further magnified by these meetings. I arranged her seat between me and her Aunt Rebecca, fully planning to shower a little extra love on her that night. We were settled at the table in record speed. All the playing outside had made everyone hungry.

"Let's hold hands," Mike encouraged. Everyone grabbed the hand next to them, and Honey volunteered to pray. Her sweet voice fit her name. She thanked God for things that seemed so simple to the rest of us, but as I looked around the table at the people I loved, I thought of the hurt of addiction, homelessness, and foster care, and Honey's prayer of thanksgiving rang true and clear. Grace slipped her delicate long fingers between mine. I squeezed three times, and she squeezed back three times—it was our secret code that meant "I love you."

Dinner was fantastic. As I finished my plate of food and pushed it away from me, I had a moment to sit back and observe the smiling faces of those I loved deeply. Laughter filled the room, and for a moment, the hard parts of our life fell away. Manny relaxed into a deep conversation with Derek about engines. It sounded like gibberish to me, but my heart felt full. My kids' birth family showered them with attention and included Grace in their loving embrace. They never failed to bring each child a little something. This time, it was silly putty in three different colors. Despite her sorrow, Grace smiled and accepted her gift.

Once everyone was finished, we divided the cleanup just as we had during my childhood. Conversations ebbed and flowed around us. Children cleared tables and giggled, got distracted, and returned to the task at hand until the house was back to normal. Rebecca and I produced three pies. Hers were apple and peach. I have absolutely no skill for baking, but my sister is a pro. Her pies were not only delicious; they were beautiful. I hated to cut into them, but the line of greedy children forming in my kitchen convinced me it was time.

After pie was served, we met up in the family room to choose a Christmas movie. That year, we settled on *Charlie Brown Christmas*. Before we knew it, the sun said goodnight and so did the kids. As the long day took its toll, Luna was the first to fall asleep. Rebecca carried her to her bed. Aaron was next. His mom kissed him on the forehead and so did I, and then Mike carried him to his bed. The movie ended, and everyone else brushed their teeth without a fight.

We said our goodbyes to Christine and Aaron's family, and the rest of the adults and Manny met back up in the kitchen. We had to agree, it was a nearly perfect day.

We picked a board game to play. Ticket to Ride was my favorite, and despite my mock confidence at winning a third year in a row, I knew it was possible that someone would break my winning streak. Manny opted out and settled into the couch to watch some TV. I set up the pieces at the kitchen table and passed out the train pieces and cards. Manny glanced over a few times. Mike noticed and invited him once more to play. He inched toward the table and then asked about the rules. "Seems easy enough," he said with a shrug after we had finished explaining.

"Be prepared to be defeated," I warned him.

"Please, someone beat her, please!" Derek begged.

Manny just smiled. The game went on until much later than we intended to stay up. Manny was the victor by far. We were all impressed, but he was shy about the win and took in the victory with grace.

The Friday after Thanksgiving is a tradition for me and my sister. We woke up early and left the house to go "Christmas shopping." We usually didn't acquire any presents though. We started with a leisurely stop at a coffee shop, then browsed a local bookstore, and finally ended up at a cute little bistro for lunch. Occasionally we stumbled on a gift for one of the kids, but mostly the day was just about being sisters. The guys were at home with the kids, but we didn't feel bad for them. Their turn to go out was coming that evening.

Rebecca and I found the perfect seat in the tiny restaurant. Large windows flooded us with warm sunshine despite the chilly temperatures outside. I slid my coat off my shoulders and placed it on the back of the chair. Rebecca did the same and signaled the waitress with a smile, letting her know we were ready to order. My soup arrived in a cobalt-blue bowl that matched the pattern on the curtains. A philodendron elegantly curled around the curtain rod, trailing its way toward the edge of my chair. I pointed to the house-plant, reminding my sister that we used to have time to remember to water things.

She laughed. "I wish my house looked like this," she said with a sigh.

"Me too," I agreed. We sipped our second and third cups of cof-fee, savoring our bowls of soup and delicate croissants. Then the phone rang. We looked at each other with the understanding that whatever was said on this call, our lunch date was probably over. I picked up the phone.

"So everything is fine—we're just wondering how to get blood out of the carpet." It was Mike.

"I'm not even going to ask," I responded and then gave him the instructions on where to find the peroxide and told him to use cold water and paper towels. Rebecca and I finished our lunch and returned home to survey the damage.

The house wasn't too bad, and the blood had come from a previ-ously loose tooth that was knocked free during a particularly rowdy game of Twister. The child with the missing tooth was proud of his new gap-toothed grin, and all was well.

Mike and Derek decided to take Manny to the skate park. "This kid deserves some time away from the little kids. He's been a champ today." Rebecca and I agreed. Aaron and his cousin Everett begged to go too, and finally, the dads agreed to let them tag along. Manny seemed excited to have an audience.

They hadn't been gone an hour when Rebecca and I realized that Christine wasn't playing with the other kids. I found her in her room with her face down on the pillow. "I don't want to be a middle child," she screamed into her pillow when I placed my hand on her back. I couldn't quite understand her and asked her again what was wrong. She rolled over and nearly spit in my face. "I don't want to be a middle child! You always have to bring new kids home, and this time Manny thinks he can be the oldest." She said "Manny" as if it had four syllables. She continued, "Why did you adopt me, anyway? Why? You don't want me; you and Dad just want Manny and Grace and Aaron."

I was confused and a little angry. I knew I should be understanding and sympathetic, but I was feeling attacked and sad. Rebecca peered around the corner and pointed to herself then shrugged her shoulders in a gesture that asked if I'd like her to take a turn. I nodded. Rebecca stepped in, and I joined the other kids in the kitchen to make another craft. If there is something that brings me joy in life, it's a good craft. After a while, Rebecca and Christine came down the stairs. Rebecca asked if it was okay to go to the grocery store, and I agreed.

The kids and I made some of the best fall leaf rubbings and stuck them all over the walls of the kitchen in a lovely autumn display. Christine and Rebecca walked back through the doors carrying bags of groceries and laughing. I raised my eyebrows at Rebecca, expressing my shock at the change. They unloaded cake decorating supplies and announced that they would need the kitchen for a while. Grace and Luna took the opportunity to ask for a movie, and we left the kitchen.

As I was walking out of the room, Christine grabbed me from behind and hugged my waist. "I'm sorry I yelled at you, Mommy."

I turned around and patted her on the head. "It's okay. I'm glad you had a good talk with Aunt Rebecca," I said.

"I did! Did you know she's a middle child?" she exclaimed.

I nodded. "Yes, I did know that. She won't let any of us forget it either!" I joked with a wink toward my sister. Christine and Rebecca worked together in the kitchen while I played with Grace and Luna. Derek and Mike stayed at the park with the boys until they practically fell from exhaustion. I wished we could have a community like this every day.

Part 4

THE SORROW
OF WINTER

16

STRETCHED THIN

On December 5, Frank called again. "Angelica was released from detention today." He didn't waste time getting to the point. "I…well, we…she, um…she needs a place to stay."

I interrupted him. "Who is Angelica?" as the words came out of my mouth, I realized what was happening. Manny's sister. I nearly smacked myself in the forehead.

Rolling my eyes at myself, I listened to Frank's explanation. "Angelica is out on probation for now. I would typically look for another home for her, but I think maybe this time she would really do better with Manny. She will have IOP for the next two weeks, and then she can receive home-based counseling. Her treatment team meets tomorrow. I think it would be good if you could be there too…"

He trailed off long enough for me to ask what IOP was.

He apologized for being scatterbrained and explained that IOP stands for intensive outpatient. Angelica was in a drug rehabilitation program in addition to her involvement with the Department of Child Services and now probation. I mentally ticked off the details I would need to add to our daily schedule. It felt overwhelming, and

I wasn't sure I could manage another high-needs child. But I also thought about Manny and his concern for his sister.

"Okay, we can do it. Where do you need me to get her?" The phone went nearly silent and I thought I'd dropped the call. "Frank?"

I heard the phone shuffle then his voice returned on the line. "Sorry again. So about that, I'm actually leaving the courthouse now, and I can head straight to your house."

I closed my eyes and tried to reorient myself. "Okay?" I said it as more of a question than answer.

Frank pulled into the driveway 30 minutes after our call. In the half hour between, I made up the bed in Christine's bedroom. She was hoping to get it back soon, but we hadn't gotten around to moving her bed and dresser back over there. She was generous enough to share her space when Juniper and Jonathan were with us too. I was so proud of her selflessness.

I felt a little sick to my stomach as I made the bed up for another child. I knew Christine would feel sad. I found a pair of jersey knit sheets in the hall closet and pulled them tightly around the bed. I hoped Angelica would like the light yellow Christine had chosen for the walls just a year earlier. I stood in the doorway and surveyed the room. "Not bad," I said to myself.

The doorbell rang, and I ran down the steps to get it. Frank's mouth was grinning, but his eyes were not. He looked tired. Behind him stood a petite, dark-haired girl. She was staring at her red-and-white checked converse and pulling at the strings on her frayed jeans. She peered up at me through her bangs briefly and then quickly returned to fidgeting.

Angelica held one garbage bag that was about half full in her left arm. Her backpack was slung over the same shoulder. On second glance, her dark hair revealed itself to be a light strawberry blonde at the roots. Her skin was pale and strikingly flawless. Her ear was pierced from top to bottom, and I lost count as I numbered the earrings. Her bottom lip was pierced on the left side, and two studs were placed in the skin on her chin. She stuck her tongue out absently and rubbed her tongue piercing along her upper lip. I have to say, I was impressed with her commitment to her look.

"Well, come on in, Angelica. It's nice to meet you."

She rolled her eyes in an exaggerated motion. "It's Angel."

I kept my tone even. "It's nice to meet you, Angel." She flicked her eyes upward one more time. I stuck my hand out to her to shake and waited. She did not shake my hand. I stood there another moment, keeping my arm steady. She glanced up once more and I smiled. She looked down at her shoes and, without meeting my gaze, offered her hand loosely for me to grasp. I shook her hand gently and reached for her bags. She dropped them on the floor. I left them there.

Turning to Frank, I began the business of gathering details. "What school will she attend?" I asked first. Frank informed me that Angel was currently expelled from school. IOP would replace her school day. He wrote the address down for me on the notebook I pulled from a drawer in the kitchen.

Turning to Angel, I asked, "What do you want me to know?"

She sighed and said, "I won't be here long."

I took my opportunity. "I know this is hard. I'm sorry you have to be here. You can feel free to watch some TV until it's time to get the kids from school." I handed her the remote and turned my attention back to Frank. He helped me gather her Medicaid number, her mother's name, her doctor's name, and the name and number of her probation officer. The list filled most of the first page of the legal pad. My pen ran out of ink, and I shuffled through the junk drawer looking for another. I tried three, unsuccessfully scratching them onto the paper and then throwing them out, before settling

on one of Grace's sparkle gel pens. I finished Angel's notes with a little glittery flair. I kind of wished I would have begun with that pen.
The notes did look a little less depressing in that color. I placed the
notebook on the counter and walked Frank to the door.

"Good luck," he said as I closed the door behind him. I could see
that we were going to need it, but I still thought it was a little odd
for him to admit it.

Angel reluctantly moved from the couch a few hours after Frank
left. She had been watching a marathon of MTV. I wondered if
I should be grateful for the year of cable TV my mother-in-law
had given us for Christmas the previous year. For the time being,
I was glad that Angel had something to do. She seemed content to
plant herself in front of the stream of poorly acted "reality." I secretly
found it more enjoyable than the Disney Channel my younger kids
begged to watch every morning before school. She shuffled with
painfully slow movements toward the car. I looked at my watch dis-
creetly, not wanting this to be our first battle. Luckily, I still had time
to get in the back of the pickup line to retrieve the kids before heading to Manny's school. Angel climbed into the back seat. I hadn't
expected that but understood her need for space. I glanced in the
rearview mirror to see her slip an earbud into each ear and shift to
stare out the window. Despite her icy demeanor, she was just a child.
I reached up to turn the mirror back, not wanting to intrude on her
private moment. Just then she looked up and locked eyes with me.
We both turned away.

Christine, Grace, and Aaron raced each other to the car even
though they had been warned multiple times by the principal to
walk. They tumbled inside, climbing over each other and flinging
backpacks, each one vying for my attention. Abruptly, the commotion stopped, and all three children turned to stare at the stranger
in the back seat.

"What are you doing here?" Aaron asked without tact.

Angel looked sideways at him but said nothing.

Aaron corrected himself. "Hi, I'm Aaron, who are you?" He looked up at me for approval and I gave him a thumbs-up.

"Are all of your kids black?" She said the words as a question, but her tone was sharp.

We had not yet left the pickup line, so I put the car in park and turned around to face her. "Is that going to be a problem for you?" My tone matched hers. Aaron's eyes darted from my face to hers and back.

Christine folded her arms across her chest and raised the level of sass. "Yeah, is that a problem?"

Angel jutted her chin out, her mouth a resolute line. I waited. "No," she whispered.

Christine seemed satisfied, and so did Aaron. Grace looked out her window without saying a word.

"Great then," I continued cheerfully. "Angel, this is Christine, Grace, and Aaron." I pointed to each child. "Kids, this is Angel. She's going to stay with us for a little while." I put the car back in drive and gently took my foot off the brake.

We rolled up outside of the high school just as clubs were releasing. Students swarmed the parking lot, library, and nearby coffee shop. I waved a small wave when I spotted Manny. I didn't want to embarrass him, but I was already learning that embarrassment was not something in Manny's vocabulary. He grinned when he saw the 12-passenger van, and I had to laugh at his willingness to join our family's odd ways without hesitation.

Aaron nearly jumped out of the roof with excitement over seeing Manny. Over the last few weeks, Manny and Aaron really hit it off. Manny was kind to all the kids, but Aaron idolized him. It warmed my heart to think of the patience Manny showed with Aaron's endless Lego projects and unfiltered questions. Manny claimed the front seat and began to tell me that he needed me to get his phone from the dean. He had lost it for playing with it in class again. I realized that meant he hadn't gotten my earlier text about Angel.

Before I could explain everything he had missed, he saw her sitting in the back seat. "Hi, Angel." His inflection changed ever so slightly. A tense, protective, almost paternal mood took over the carefree Manny we had come to expect. "I'm glad you're out. Who's your probation officer?"

Angel looked him straight in the face. "You're not my parent, Manny, so don't try to be."

He didn't even flinch. His eyes blinked once, and he replied, "Don't ruin this for me, Angel. I've got a good thing here."

She rolled her eyes before looking out the window again and snapped back, "Oh, I won't ruin it for precious you, don't worry." There was no recovery for the mood of our car, so I turned on the radio before clicking the left turn signal and heading toward home.

When we got home, Manny went straight to his room, Grace and Christine took their snacks and a box of craft supplies into the dining room, and Aaron hung his head, looking like a lost puppy. A twinge of regret blossomed in my chest, and I crouched next to Aaron, offering a squeeze. He accepted, and I held him tight. "I think Manny's feeling a little sad. Would you like to make him a card? You are the best artist I know."

Aaron's face brightened, and he trotted off to find his sisters and their treasure trove of construction paper and smelly markers. I double-checked to see that they were settled and went to find Angel. She was sitting in the middle of her new room with her legs tucked under her chin. She looked small.

"Hey," I said and then paused. "Your laundry is done. Did Frank say when we could pick up the rest?" She shook her head almost imperceptibly. "Well, I will call him first thing in the morning. No problem." I went immediately into problem-solver mode. It really was my greatest strength.

Angel began to cry. I froze. Fighting off panic, I looked at the ceiling and then at the window, hoping that some sort of help would come. It didn't. I tried not to panic. Moments like these always left me feeling inadequate. Should I hug her? Should I pat her on the back? How long was I supposed to let her cry? Should I ask her something? I did not know what to do. Then I made a random guess and went for it. I crouched next to her, close but not touching.

I put my hand out toward her and said, "I'm really sorry. I can't imagine what this is like. What can I do to help?"

Without looking up, she answered through sniffles, "We were living with my mom's boyfriend. He told us to get out and threw our stuff on the lawn. My mom made us leave. I couldn't get my things. They're gone." She wiped away a tear and then took a joking tone. "It doesn't matter anyway," she said in a lighthearted voice that sounded forced. "It's not like it's the first time."

An invisible wall went up around her and I moved to give her space. "That sounds like a big deal to me. I'm sorry that happened. I'll bring your stuff up from the laundry room. When you're up to it, we can look around the house, and I'll show you where everything is." She turned away, and I closed the door almost all the way as I left her room.

I stuck my head into Manny's room and told him I was just checking in and to take all the time he needed. He too did not respond. I was losing any hope that I might be good at fostering teens. After returning downstairs to check on the younger kids, I sent a text to Mike asking what our budget was for a quick trip to the store for some teenage girl essentials. We settled on a number together, and I began to form a plan.

Manny made his exodus around 6:00 p.m. He sulked through the kitchen, grabbing an apple from the fruit basket next to the sink. He shrugged at me and then moved toward the mudroom. His skateboard was propped next to the overflowing basket of shoes. With no explanation, he left the house. I called after him, reminding him that dinner would be ready soon. The door slammed when I was midsentence.

Mike pulled into the driveway just as I returned to the kitchen. He called tentatively from the mudroom, "Hello? I just passed Manny on the sidewalk—is everything okay?" He came into the kitchen and raised his eyebrows at me.

I shrugged once and gestured to Angel, who had moved back to the couch. "Mike, this is Angel," I said brightly. Angel didn't look up. Christine, Grace, and Aaron rounded the corner and flung themselves into their daddy's arms. He squeezed them tightly and kissed their foreheads. Aaron proudly waved the card he had created for Manny in his daddy's face, so close that some of the glitter sprinkled off onto Mike's nose. Mike took it from him carefully. It read, "I hp u flll bttr. AARON." Mike carefully sounded out the misspelled words. "I hope you feel better? Is that right, Aaron?" Aaron nodded and ran upstairs to put the card on Manny's bed.

Dinner was ready, and suddenly I realized I couldn't remember the last time I'd eaten a meal. My stomach rumbled in response to my realization. "I'm starving. Come on, everyone, let's head to the table."

Everyone came running and even Angel moved tentatively toward the kitchen. I turned my back, leaning one elbow on the counter, and quickly sent a text to Manny to tell him it was time to eat but heard no reply. Mike and I exchanged another glance but continued toward the dinner table anyway. Angel stood awkwardly next to my chair and I realized she didn't know where to sit. I felt an ache in my chest as I observed her hard expression falter slightly while her eyes scanned the table.

"Right here," Mike responded, quickly pulling a chair out for her. She glanced around once more and then sat slowly. Aaron was the first to dig in, as always. His hand was poised over the plate of spaghetti and meatballs.

"Wait," Christine warned, "we always pray first."

Aaron stuck his tongue out at her and set his fork down. "You're not my mom," he responded.

Mike stepped in. "That's true. Christine, you are not his mom. However, Aaron, we always pray before dinner. Who would like to pray tonight?" Grace raised her hand, and I was surprised. Grace was shy even at home and usually didn't volunteer to talk out loud. We bowed our heads and closed our eyes. I allowed one eye to creep open so I could watch my children. Aaron's fingers were folded just above his steaming plate of pasta, and his eyes were watching the swirl of steam trail upward toward his fingers. I shifted my gaze to Angel and saw that her eyes were wide open watching all of us. She caught my glance, and I winked.

Manny didn't return home for dinner. We assigned each child an after-dinner chore. Even Angel took hers without complaint. Mike and I stepped into the hallway to talk. Dishes clinked into the sink, food was scraped into the dog's dish. Christine swished the broom past us at least three times while we talked, but the floor didn't really look swept.

"Hey, Christine, are your ears burning?" we said jokingly in unison.

"No," she responded flatly, but the warning reminded her that it was not her conversation.

"It's too much to tell right now," I whispered. "Angel and Manny got in a fight in the car. Manny was really upset. His whole demeanor changed when he saw her. I really thought it would be a good thing for them to be together, but now I'm just not sure."

Mike listened and nodded. "Should I go find him? It's getting really dark."

I was beginning to feel worried. I had intended to give him space, but I really thought he would have returned by now.

Mike grabbed a coat and hat. He shoved the car keys in his pocket and slipped out the door. The kids finished their chores quickly and ran toward the stairs to get their pajamas on.

"Where's Daddy going?" Grace asked with concern when she heard the engine start.

"Daddy's going to look for Manny. He was feeling a little upset today and just needed a little time away."

Grace's face creased, and tears welled up. "It's really cold though."

I patted her head. "I know, but Manny is smart. He's just fine, I'm sure." I was not so sure, and the knot that had formed in my stomach was tightening.

Angel was back on the couch. "He's at Sawyer Park," she said flatly.

I turned my head toward her. "How do you know?" I asked.

"That's always where he goes," she answered.

"He walked?" I asked again.

She nodded, and I picked up the phone to call Mike. He answered on the first ring. "Try Sawyer Park," I said quickly. He had the same questions I did, but we both agreed that it was the most likely place for him to be.

Mike arrived at the park a few minutes later, and as he pulled into the space closest to the fence surrounding the skate park, he saw a figure in the glow of the streetlamp. Putting the car in park, he watched for a minute. Placing the keys back in his pocket, he shut the car door and walked briskly toward the gate. As he moved closer, he could tell it was Manny. He was alone. He didn't look up at first but must have noticed the car arrive. Mike put his hands into his pockets to keep warm and watched. Manny was really good at skateboarding.

Finally, Manny came over to where Mike stood. "Sorry," he mumbled.

Mike shook his head. "No need to be sorry. You just have to tell us, okay?"

Manny nodded and then opened the gate to exit the park. Mike patted him once on the back and then said cheerfully, "You must be freezing. Come on, you can tell me about your day on the way home. Kristin made spaghetti."

Manny did talk on the way home. He shared about his relationship with Angel and their mom. For a few moments, he was transparent, and Mike didn't want to interrupt, so he just listened. They pulled into the driveway and slammed two doors shut. I could hear from the kitchen and was flooded with relief.

Once Manny and Mike returned home, I went to Angel's room and knocked on the door. "Hey, would you like to go to the store with me? I need to get a few things, and I think you could use a few new clothes until we get all of your things sorted out."

She looked surprised. "Really?"

We didn't talk on the way to the store. We pulled in front of Target, and I pulled out an envelope with some cash inside. "Mike and I have a little extra money we want you to spend on clothes. It's not a lot, but it should get you started." She looked at the amount and raised her eyebrows a little and stiffly thanked me. We found the clearance section and grabbed a few shirts and a jacket. Pants were a little trickier, but she finally found two pairs. I called that a success.

Finally, we stopped in the underwear section. "I know this is embarrassing, but everyone needs underwear," I said as cheerfully as possible. She laughed a little and we picked out five pairs. Grabbing a package of socks, we completed our shopping trip and started for home.

As we pulled into the driveway, she looked at me with a look I hadn't seen yet—gratitude, perhaps, or maybe it was surprise. "I thought you were taking me back to DCS."

I turned my head toward her as I put the car in park. "Why would I do that?"

She shook her head and whispered, "That's what usually happens."

I thought for a minute. "Not here, okay?" She nodded, but I could tell she didn't believe me. To be truthful, I wasn't sure I believed me. I wasn't sure I was equipped to give Angel what she needed.

17

BROKEN BONES, BROKEN HEARTS

The month of December flew by. Angel struggled with finding her place in our home. Sometimes she was a loving big sister to the girls, and sometimes she would shout at them to just leave her alone. Her ever-changing moods kept our emotions on a constant roller coaster. The uncertainty took a toll, especially on Grace, who longed for a special big sister. The tension was compounded by the fact that we found out two weeks after her arrival that she had been sneaking out of her intensive outpatient program and tested positive for marijuana. The director informed me at pickup that I would need to attend each session with her.

I raised my eyebrows in shock and gestured to the three children in the back seat. "I have other children."

The director shrugged her shoulders. "I can't babysit Angel. If she doesn't have an adult with her, she can't complete the program."

I felt furious but bit my tongue and told Angel to get in the car immediately. She obeyed. On the ride home, I did not say one word to her. I called Frank and explained the situation. He asked to speak with Angel, and I handed her the phone. All I heard for the next five minutes was "Mm-hm…yes…no…uh-huh." Without saying goodbye, she flung her hand toward me, and I plucked the phone from it. Frank told me he would call her probation officer and the IOP director and see what he could work out. He promised to call me back later that evening. I was about to hang up when he said one more thing: "Hey, before you go…Hang in there with Angel. You guys are good for her—she just doesn't know it yet."

I smiled and replied, "Okay, thanks. I'll talk to you later." I wasn't quite sure what to make of the whole situation. The rest of the ride was quiet. Even the little kids seemed to understand that I was not happy.

Later that night, after the little kids were in bed, Angel pulled up a chair at the kitchen table while I was finishing up the dishes. "I'm sorry about IOP," she whispered.

"I am too," I responded firmly and without much feeling.

"I'll help out around the house when we get home."

I didn't believe her, but I answered positively anyway. "I think that would be a very good start."

The next-door neighbor agreed to get the kids off the bus each day, and Frank convinced Angel's probation officer and IOP director to allow me to leave 45 minutes early with her to get the other kids from school on the condition that Angel participated fully in each session. I couldn't guarantee she would, but I felt that she deserved a shot at completing the program. Mike was able to get out of work early one of the days as well, and that left the kids with only three afternoons at the neighbor's house.

The first day I attended IOP, I was angry. I couldn't stop thinking about how much time this was taking away from me and my family. But by day three, I began to enjoy the alone time with Angel, and as I listened in on the sessions, I came to know her and understand her story a little better. She occasionally glanced my way to see if I was listening. I made a big show of reading my book.

One day, during the sharing part of the class, she divulged that her first memory of her parents getting high was when she was in kindergarten. They didn't come to her play at school, and when she got off the bus at the end of the day, she was heartbroken. She let herself into the house and found both of her parents passed out. Manny sent her to her room, but she didn't go. She just kept shaking them and yelling at them to wake up. They didn't. Someone called the ambulance, but she didn't know who. Her parents finally woke up and talked to the cops. Then a caseworker took the kids away. It was her first time in foster care. She glanced at me again, but this time I forgot to look away. It was too late to disguise my sadness. She didn't talk to me on the way home that night, and I didn't have the right words for her either.

Angel graduated from IOP just in time for Christmas. We had a celebration that rivaled any high school graduation party. We invited our friends and cooked all of Angel's favorite foods. Each of the kids got to pick a special treat for dessert as a reward for their flexibility the last few weeks. Even Manny seemed happy and didn't criticize Angel for the entire evening.

With only a few days till Christmas, Mike and I scrambled to complete the shopping and decorating that had been pushed aside. Mike is the best at gift giving, and despite the short time frame, he planned thoughtful gifts for each child. He went a little overboard for Manny and Angel, but we both felt that it was a small price to pay for this one special day with them.

Christmas morning dawned bright and early, as it does in most homes with small children. Aaron was the first to burst through our bedroom door, quickly followed by Grace and Christine. Mike and

I pretended to be too sleepy to get up. Mike rubbed his eyes and looked at the kids in mock confusion. "Why are you waking me up? There's nothing planned today. Mom and I are going to sleep in till ten. Go back to bed."

Finally, the three kids couldn't take the joke anymore. They started pulling our arms and legs to get us out of bed, giggling and shouting joyfully, "It's Christmas!" Mike and I looked at each other and then jumped out of bed, racing the kids to the stairs. At the top, we paused and reminded them that we always go down together on Christmas morning. They nodded and pointed impatiently at Angel's and Manny's doors. We nodded with permission that they could go wake the big kids up. They cheered and pulled the same nonsense with the truly sleepy teens. Manny and Angel were less enthusiastic than we had been, but they played along.

Once all five of them were sitting on the stairs, we took the obligatory Christmas morning picture and then let them run to the fireplace to check their stockings. Manny and Angel hung back with their stockings on their laps and just watched. As the little kids opened each of their gifts, they threw the paper aside, admired their present, and then quickly ran to each parent initiating a hug and a thank-you.

Our tradition seemed normal to us, but when we looked at the big kids, they watched with confusion. I whispered, "You don't have to hug anyone if you don't want to, okay?" They both nodded.

When it was their turn to open gifts, they were subdued. They each tore the paper off carefully and placed it to the side. They politely thanked us for each gift, but their smiles never quite met their eyes. Mike and I enjoyed the day, but something nagged at our hearts every time we revisited the memory of their faces.

It wasn't until years later, when Manny and Angel were adults, that they told us about that Christmas from their perspective. They admitted that they were happy and excited to be spending the day with us and the kids. They laughed at memories of Aaron rolling himself in leftover paper and offering himself up to each of us as "the best present ever." Then they recalled the feeling of something they couldn't put into words as teenagers. The feeling of being lost, of not quite fitting in. The feeling that if they fully enjoyed the day with us, somehow, they were cheating on their parents. Mike and I nodded in understanding at their perspective. They told us that the Christmas before the one they spent with us, their mom was strung out the entire day. Their dad had been gone for years, and their mom had forgotten to buy gifts. They spent the day watching TV and eating ramen noodles. They laughed at the memory, but even a decade later, their expressions told a story of pain.

January and February were unseasonably warm for Indiana. Manny met up with friends nearly every day after school at the skate park. Angel was back in school and doing well. The school lifted her restriction from riding the bus, and my time felt more manageable again. Christine, Grace, and Aaron settled in as well.

One day, I picked the smaller kids up from school and settled them in for an after-school snack. Temperatures had dropped while they were in school, but I had already given Manny permission to stay after and go to the skate park. Aaron's fingers were sticky with peanut butter and bananas, and I realized this too late as I passed him his spelling sheet and a marker. Peanut butter was smeared all over the crisp white sheet, and Christine wrinkled her nose in disgust. With one eye on the clock, I grabbed for a paper towel and a wet rag. I ran the rag over his face and hands and then kissed his forehead before attempting to clean the homework paper. Aaron jutted a small finger past my view toward the window. "Snow!"

Sure enough, flurries of white swirled just outside the window. Grace, who typically escaped inside a book immediately after school, set her book on the table and stared out the window, mes-merized. We watched for a while in complete silence.

My phone buzzed across the table, startling all four of us. I grabbed the phone and stared at the unknown number. I almost didn't answer it and then realized that Manny's phone was broken. I clicked the green button and held the phone to my ear. "Mrs. Berry, this is Manny's friend. We're at the skate park and, um, I think he broke his arm. It looks pretty bad."

I nearly dropped the phone before answering. "Do we need to call an ambulance?"

The caller assured me he had suffered worse without a doctor. I did not feel reassured but agreed to come take a look myself and decide since we were only a few blocks away. "Okay, hang on, I'll be right there." I gestured to the kids to get in the car, and thankfully, they didn't argue. Sensing the urgency in my tone, Christine began helping Aaron with his coat and then motioned for all three of them to get to the car. Normally, I would reassure her that she didn't need to be the extra mama, but on this day, I was grateful for the addi-tional set of hands.

We made it to the park in record time. I pulled into a space that wasn't meant for parking, but I didn't care. I threw the car into park and turned to the three younger children. "Do not move. I am not kidding—stay put." They nodded solemnly. I hated to scare them, but this was no time for coddling. I ran toward the crowd of peo-ple gathered at the entrance to the skate park. The teenagers moved quickly out of my way as I approached and revealed a grimacing Manny sitting on the bench. He cradled his right arm in his left and moved his hand just enough to reveal that the right arm was bent at a disturbingly odd angle. I swallowed hard to avoid vomiting or passing out, two things I have been known to do in an emergency.

I took my coat off and draped it around the teen. "Can you walk to the car?" I asked. He nodded in response and rose carefully. As we reached the passenger side of the van, he turned to his friends and gave a big smile. I just shook my head. One of his friends shouted after us, "Don't worry, I caught it on video—it was awesome!" I nearly threw up again. Manny settled into his seat, and I reached across him to buckle his seat belt. As it clicked, I looked up at him and laughed awkwardly. "Well, I guess I never got to buckle you in as a baby, so here's my chance." He laughed too and then winced.

We were two blocks from the hospital when I realized we were supposed to get Angel in a few minutes. I called frantically to all my neighbors to see if someone could get her. Finally, I reached my friend Nicole, who happened to be working from home that day. She sounded groggy, and I felt terrible for disturbing her. She had a toddler sick and in bed, but when she heard what happened, she didn't hesitate. "I'll be there as fast as I can," she assured me.

I called Angel, but she wasn't out of class. I left a message and worried that she wouldn't get it. Manny got quieter and quieter as we turned into the hospital. I put the car in park as close to the door as possible. The snow was sticking, and it was difficult to see the parking spaces in the already full parking lot. I reached over and unbuckled Manny's belt and turned to the back seat to thank the kids for working so quickly to get in the car earlier and to get out of the car now. It was such a relief that they all knew how to work their own car seats.

Manny and I walked quickly to the sliding doors, and the three younger kids followed like ducklings. My phone rang in my pocket, and I reached quickly to get it. It was Angel, her high-pitched voice shrill with worry. "Where are you? You didn't get me!"

"Wait, did you get my voice mail?" She confirmed that she did not, and her tone began to quiet. I stood with four children in front of the registration desk and tried to calm Angel while a nurse tapped her pen impatiently on the table, waiting for me to get off the phone. I ignored her.

"I would never forget you, Angel. Miss Nicole is on her way. Look for her burgundy minivan. Manny is okay. His arm is broken, but he's doing fine. Mike or I will get you soon, okay?"

I could hear her take a deep breath. "I'm sorry I yelled at you," she apologized.

"It's okay. Everything is fine, I'll see you soon." We hung up, and the nurse glared at me. I clenched my jaw and composed myself before explaining why we were there. She took our information and showed us to the waiting room.

The waiting room was packed. I worried that Manny couldn't wait in pain much longer. I also worried that we were going to take some unneeded germs home with us. The man sitting next to us was pale and sweating. He sneezed and coughed and only occasionally covered his mouth. I moved Aaron to my lap and encouraged Christine and Grace to get some hand sanitizer.

We were finally called back to intake. The nurse who took his vitals, height, and weight was much nicer than the one at the front desk, and I was immediately relieved. She could see that Manny was in pain and got him quickly into a room. She offered the little kids popsicles. I chuckled a little at the absurdity of eating a popsicle when the temperatures outside were plummeting. The kids jumped at the offer though, and before long, they were happily slurping sugary treats. I was wondering if they were going to get any sleep that night with all the sugar.

Manny refused anything stronger than an ibuprofen for the pain. When the nurse left, he admitted that he often worried that he might struggle with addiction like his parents. My heart broke for him, but I understood and promised to get him a lot of pillows to prop that arm up while he healed. I promised ice cream too, and he agreed that a treat would help.

Mike was hard to reach from the hospital because there was no signal. I finally had to call from a landline, and when I got through, he let me know he was leaving immediately to meet me at the hospital. He got there just as Manny was being discharged. Despite the packed waiting room, the doctors were quite efficient. We had an appointment in two days to put the solid cast on, and he was being sent home with a nicely wrapped-up arm and plenty of instructions and only enough pain killers to make it through the night. The doctor understood Manny's concerns and prescribed him just enough for the worst days of pain. Manny agreed to take the medication, and I was relieved to see him in a little less pain.

The little kids were amazing throughout the whole ordeal. Mike took them to get McDonald's while I drove Manny home to get him settled in on the couch to rest. He was asleep before I stepped out of the family room. I called Nicole to check on Angel, and it turned out that they had made some art projects while I was gone and that Angel was a budding artist. I wasn't surprised. I left the house and arrived at Nicole's a few minutes later. Angel was ready to go and tucked under her arm was a makeshift portfolio that Nicole helped her create to keep her drawings out of the weather. Once we got in the car, Angel pulled out her two favorite drawings, and I was astonished by her talent.

"Do you take art class at school?" I asked.

She shook her head. "I don't like anyone else to look at what I've drawn. I usually just keep it to myself."

"You're really good," I encouraged.

"Thanks," she replied shyly and put the drawings back in the folder. I wondered to myself if it was possible to get her into art classes somewhere.

When I got home, Mike and the kids were already upstairs completing the nighttime routine, and Manny was still sound asleep on the couch. Everyone was exhausted and quickly fell asleep. Angel retreated to her room, and Mike agreed to stay in the recliner in case Manny needed anything during the night. I was grateful and went straight to bed, nearly falling asleep before my head hit the pillow.

Manny recovered quickly. Two days after the break, he was back at school. A week later, the snow melted, and he wanted to accompany his friends to the skate park. He promised not to skate, and I relented. The air was still chilly, though spring was approaching quickly. I gave him 30 minutes and told him not one minute longer. He agreed.

That afternoon, I called around to some studios in the area that were offering art classes. They were expensive, but I found one in Indianapolis that offered discounts to low-income families. When I told the receptionist that the class was for my foster daughter, she promised to see what she could do.

Manny enjoyed himself too much and didn't want to come home. It was nice to see him feeling well. His friend shared the video with him, and at dinner that night he insisted we all watch and rewatch him breaking his arm. It was disgusting, but I forced myself not to pass out cold.

A week later, Angel was approved for a full scholarship to the art studio to take any class she wanted. Mike and could not wait to tell her all about it. We decided to tell her together at dinner one night. The kids all came home, and the night was typical. We sat down to dinner, and as I looked around the table, I marveled at how our family had changed over the winter. Angel and Manny sat down to dinner looking completely at home. They initiated conversation and participated in our prayer time.

We announced the good news to Angel just as she passed a plate of peas to Aaron and helped him scoop a spoonful onto his plate. She froze midscoop, and a smile spread across her face. "Really?" was all she managed to squeak out. She seemed hesitant to accept the news almost as if she believed we would take it away. We nodded to her, unable to contain smiles of our own. The rest of dinner was filled with happy conversation, and our night ended with hearts full. Our home felt so complete, I couldn't believe that two teenagers fit like long-missing pieces to a puzzle.

18

JOY BECOMES SORROW

A ngel was floating with excitement for the rest of the night. After dinner, we gave her the catalog. Spring classes were starting in less than three weeks, and she needed to choose a class. They all looked amazing, and we could tell it was hard for her to choose. We were so proud of her for the steps she was taking toward wise choices and healthy living, so Mike and I agreed to let her take two classes. We felt that driving to art classes would be so much more fun than hours of driving and sitting at IOP anyway. She narrowed her choices down to two just before bedtime, and Mike got online and registered her before he climbed into bed. He reached over to turn out the light and asked, "Did you ever think we would be doing something so fun with Angel?"

I rolled over and looked him right in the eye as I shook my head. "I didn't see this coming at all. I really love them, you know?"

He nodded. "I do too. They are really good kids."

We each turned our lights off and fell fast asleep.

About an hour later, Angel shook me awake. I jumped up in surprise. "What is it?" I said as I reached for my glasses.

"It's my mom. Something's wrong."

I slid my glasses over my ears and pushed the lenses up the bridge of my nose. I got out of bed, following Angel into the hallway. I turned the hall light on and squinted as my eyes adjusted to the brightness. She was shaking, and her words were jumbled.

"I didn't turn my phone in tonight. I'm sorry, I know I was supposed to. I know the caseworker said it wasn't a good idea to talk to my mom, but I've been talking to her anyway." She paused, and I nodded to encourage her to keep going. "She just called. She's high—I think she's pretty messed up. She said she woke up in the alley by Aunt Lucy's house." Angel's voice got higher and faster as she told the story. "She needs help—she needs me. I need to go, okay? I need to go get her." Angel was getting hysterical.

I shook off the last bit of sleepiness and put my hands on her shoulders. "Okay, we'll think of something."

I took Angel's phone and called her mom back. She answered on the first ring. She wasn't making a lot of sense. I explained who I was, and she started to cry. "Don't think bad of me, okay? Please don't think bad of me. I'm not always like this."

I listened and did my best to encourage her. I talked her through the ideas I had for getting help. "Can you call 911? How about your sister?" She refused any help, and I didn't know what to do. Abruptly, she hung up the phone. I stood staring at Angel, trying to think of something to say, but nothing came to me. Angel was frantically looking from me to the phone and back.

Manny's door handle turned, and he came shuffling out into the hallway to see what was going on. Angel told him, and he immediately snapped to attention. They both agreed that their mom needed help. "What do you normally do when this happens?" I asked.

"We find her wherever she is and walk her home. Sometimes she doesn't want to go, but she'll get hurt if she stays out all night. Just drive us," they pleaded.

Mike stepped into the hallway next, and Manny filled him in on what was happening. I decided to call the caseworker. He didn't answer. I called the emergency line at DCS. The caseworker on call told me there was nothing they could do.

I started to call 911, but Manny grabbed the phone from my hand. "You can't call them—they'll never let us go back!"

Finally, Mike offered to go to her neighborhood and look for her. "If I find her, I'll offer some help. Will that work?"

Manny and Angel started downstairs to grab their coats. "We can't let you go," I said with certainty. "Not while you have an open DCS case. I'll go with Mike, and you two stay with the kids. I promise we will look everywhere, and we will call you if we find her, okay?" They reluctantly agreed. Mike and I pulled coats and boots on over our pajamas and went to the car, locking the door behind us. The engine warmed quickly, and both of us were now alert.

"What are we doing?" Mike asked.

"I honestly don't know. We need to call the police," I continued. I dialed the number and gave the dispatcher all the information I knew. It wasn't much, and I immediately felt guilty for betraying the trust of the kids.

We drove toward the neighborhood, not quite knowing what we would find. I felt calm and clearheaded even though I knew I should be afraid. Manny had given us his Aunt Lucy's address, so we started there. We drove slowly up and down the streets. No police officers came. The streets on this side of town were worn and uneven. Mike dodged potholes every few feet as I strained my eyes for any sight of their mom.

"We did our best," Mike said in defeat.

"I don't know what else we can do. I feel bad for the kids, but I think we need to head back. Maybe she got herself home already," I said hopefully. I was relieved that we were off the hook. We made one last turn before heading back toward home. Mike didn't see the pothole in front of us and we hit with an epic crash. Mike winced, and I let out a gasp. Just then I saw something. "Go back." Mike looked at me with disbelief. "Go back, I think I see something." He put the car in reverse and maneuvered around the pothole, barely missing it. I squinted toward the alley. I saw a shoe and then one bare leg. "Oh no, it's her," I whispered. I looked around and didn't see anyone. The street was quiet. I rolled the window down and said tentatively, "Hello."

The person didn't move.

"We can't get out. I don't know what to do. She looks hurt," I said to Mike.

"I'm calling an ambulance—we aren't equipped to help her," Mike replied. I agreed, and he made the call.

Mike waited on the line and we sat, waiting uncomfortably. We hadn't assessed the danger before running into the situation. We didn't know if someone had done this to her or if she had passed out. The feeling of danger gripped me. Just then, I saw her move. She sat up and shielded her eyes from the headlights. I rolled my window back down. "Candy? Is that you?"

She nodded. Her eye was swollen shut and her shirt was torn. She crawled a few feet and stumbled to her feet, I flung the door open without thinking. I stepped slowly toward her. "Are you okay? What happened? It's me, Kristin."

She fell into my arms, and the stench of urine and liquor filled my nostrils. "I'm sorry I did this. I know I hurt my babies. Are my babies okay? Do you know where they are? Who are you?" She cycled through the same questions while thick tears drenched my shoulder. She wiped her nose on her hand, and the mucus glistened in the streetlight. I looked over my shoulder at Mike and made a questioning face. He shrugged his shoulders. Sirens blared in the distance, and Candy's body stiffened.

"They just want to help," I said. "You're not in trouble, you're just hurt. Okay? Please let them help you." She slumped in defeat. A police officer pulled up behind our car and turned the siren off. The lights circled eerily in the darkness. Flashes of red and blue bounced through the street and illuminated the dilapidated homes and boarded-up windows. The officer got out of his car with his gun drawn. He shined a flashlight up and down the sidewalk and into the broken windows of the house above us. Nothing. We were alone.

Soon an ambulance and fire truck pulled onto the street. Candy broke free from her embrace and started to run. She tripped over her own foot and fell to the ground with a thud. The officer reached her just as she fell. He knelt beside her, and I wondered if he was there to help or to arrest her. He talked softly to her and offered a hand.

Paramedics rushed past me and took over as the officer came to us to get our statement. We didn't have much to say, and he was done quickly. "We see her all the time. She got it pretty bad this time."

My eyebrows raised in shock. "This has happened before?"

He nodded once.

"Oh" was all I could muster.

He allowed us to talk to her as she was taken to the ambulance on a stretcher.

"Who are you?" she said again.

Mike answered, "Manny and Angel's foster parents. They were worried about you. They're safe, okay?" His voice caught in his throat.

She nodded, and her eyes filled with momentary clarity. "Thank you for what you are doing for my babies." Then she laid her head back and closed her one good eye.

We said thank you to the police and paramedics as we walked back to our car. Dazed by what we had witnessed and feeling suddenly and completely out of place, we climbed back in without another word. Mike put the car in drive and rolled right over the pothole again. I winced. The turn signal clicked, breaking the silence. We turned, and the red and blue lights disappeared behind us.

Mike drove methodically, and I stared out the window as the abandoned homes gave way to tidy rows of apartments. The car bumped over the railroad tracks, and the city streets gave way to suburban neighborhoods. "Oh," I said under my breath as I realized for the first time what the phrase "wrong side of the tracks" meant. My phone buzzed in the cupholder beside me.

"Did you find her?" the text message read.

I quickly typed back, "Yes, she's fine. She's with a doctor now. She says she loves you." I sat the phone in my lap.

Mike reached over and squeezed my hand. "I can't believe they've been through that before."

I shook my head. "I know. I just can't imagine. I guess I knew why they were in foster care, but I just didn't really understand." We rode the rest of the way home without saying a word, connected by our laced fingers and our shared experience.

We pulled into our own neighborhood just as the sun peeked over the edge of the earth. Brilliant pink filled the sky, a sharp contrast to the darkness we had witnessed just an hour earlier. Manny and Angel were asleep on the couch when we arrived back home. We woke them to let them know it was okay to go back to bed for a bit. We would call them into school late and take them once they woke.

They uncurled themselves from the couch and started for the

stairs. Then Angel turned around and grabbed both of us in a hug. She squeezed for a moment, awkwardly let go, and continued to her bedroom. I looked at Mike, who shrugged his shoulders in surprise. We set our alarms for two hours later, and I decided I would write a letter of gratitude to the school district for setting the school start time at 9:30. We knew we could squeeze in a little rest before driving the little ones to class.

The kids' mom recovered, but the incident added another charge of possession to her growing list. Things were not looking good for her. Our caseworker stopped by later that week to talk to the kids about their mom spending possible further jail time. He also told us that the judge would likely require her to spend time in a rehabilitation facility before attempting to regain custody. He wanted to know if we would be okay keeping the kids a while longer. We agreed without hesitation. The caseworker left, and we started talking about the future. Our enthusiasm was tempered only by the realization that our time with the kids came at the expense of their relationship with their mom.

The last day of winter was a stunningly springlike day. The sun burst forth with hope of the new season to come. Art class was starting for Angel the next day, and Manny had surprised us by entering a choir competition the following weekend. I added black dress shoes to the list of items to buy that day after Manny insisted he would rather die than go into a shoe store. Once everyone was settled in for the day, I headed out to run errands. I loaded the car with groceries and made a quick stop at the shoe store. Thankfully they had exactly what I needed—I was in and out of the store in less than five minutes. I started the car and immediately realized I didn't know where my phone was. I put the bag of shoes on the front seat and slid my hands carefully under the seats in search of my phone. I began to get worried when I finally felt it buzz. It had slipped between the door and the seat back. I grabbed it but missed the call. My brow wrinkled when I realized it was the caseworker. It was unusual to hear from him twice in one month, and it had only been two weeks since we saw him. I called him back immediately.

He answered right away, and his voice didn't sound quite right. He explained that Manny and Angel's mom had called in several complaints that week. She was filing an official report on us because of Manny's broken arm. She also claimed we were "poisoning their minds."

I couldn't think of what to say. I shook my head for a minute to clear the impulsive anger rising in my chest and tried to choose my words carefully. "She hasn't been to a visit in over a month," I said. "How would she know what's happening with the kids?"

Frank agreed. He was not worried about the report against us and told me there would be no investigation. That should have been good news, but I sensed there was more. Frank cleared his throat and told me the rest. "Mom has convinced Aunt Lucy to take the kids. She passed the background check. Since she's a relative, she doesn't have to take any training. The court approved her today."

He fell silent, and I could contain my feelings no longer. My thoughts came rushing out in a jumble. "Aunt Lucy? Where has she been for the last three months? She has never been to a visit or made a phone call—nothing. The kids have been alone in all of this. There was no family around. Why now? What about Angel's art classes? Will she take her to those? What about Manny's competition?" I trailed off, my heart feeling like it was splitting in two. Then I asked the most important question: "When?"

Frank swallowed once before answering, his gulp audible through the phone. "Tonight. Lucy will come get them tonight."

I reached over toward the shoes and lifted the bag. "But the contest...but the art class," I whispered.

"I know," Frank returned. "The court is pushing for families first."

I put my head in my hands, feeling crazy. "I believe in families first too!" I nearly shouted. "I believe in families, but this family hurt the kids I love. How can this be right?"

Frank told me he was busy and wouldn't be able to be there, but we could expect Aunt Lucy by five. Frank had nothing further to say, and we hung up. I balled the handle of the shopping bag in my fist and flung it toward the back seat. The shoes toppled out, and the bag crinkled, slipping beneath the groceries.

I drove toward home in silence. I needed to call Mike; I needed to tell the kids. All the kids. This change would hurt so badly. Remembering what had happened after the sudden loss of our foster son, I made the decision to get the kids from school. I called Mike and changed direction, driving to the high school instead.

His first reaction was to be practical. "Well, okay. This is okay. We'll miss them, but maybe it will be good for them. Maybe she's just been busy the last few months." His voice cracked, and I felt the tears well up again. He only had one meeting in the afternoon, and it was something he could accomplish over the phone. He decided to come home so we could help the kids get themselves ready together. Manny appeared at the front office just moments after I arrived. His eyes shifted past me as if he were expecting something to happen. I thanked the receptionist and walked in silence toward the parked car. Manny had learned to buckle his own seat belt despite the thick blue cast on his arm. As he clicked it into place, he started the conversation.

"My mom sent a text this morning. Are we really going to Lucy's house?"

I nodded.

He sat in silence while we crossed the street and entered the middle school parking lot. Angel was waiting on the small plastic couch in the office. The look on her face told me she already knew what was happening. She followed me to the car but didn't say a word.

Finally, Manny broke the silence. "Are you okay?" he asked as he looked toward the back seat.

Angel shrugged. "I want to go with her. She's our real family anyway."

Her words hurt a little despite my resolve to support her no matter what. I answered, "You'll be fine there, Angel. You can call us anytime, you know that? Anytime."

Her voice became hard as she replied, "I don't need you. I'm not going to call."

Mike agreed to pick the little kids up early so he could tell them before they came home. I didn't envy him that job. Manny and Angel started packing right away when they got home. They were somber, and I did my best to lighten the mood. I made some break-and-bake cookies and joked about my complete inability to bake real food.

Manny said, "That's okay, I like this kind better anyway."

I knew that couldn't possibly be true, but I appreciated the sentiment. The younger kids tumbled through the door, and despite the tears, they were lured into the kitchen by the smell of warm cookies. I called all the kids to the table. They came quickly, but Angel was distracted. "I just want us to have a little time together before Aunt Lucy gets here. Okay?" I was having a hard time getting the words out, and Mike took over.

"We know this feels sad and exciting and hard all at the same time."

The kids nodded, and then Angel said, "Can I finish packing

now?" We nodded, and everyone dispersed. Aaron brought his Legos to the family room and began to spread pieces everywhere. Grace grabbed a book and curled up on the couch. Christine started on her homework. Manny was packed and ready to go in a few moments. He plopped his duffel bag on the floor next to the door, and then went out to get his skateboard. The clock ticked loudly, and time seemed to creep along.

At 5:15, I became hopeful that they wouldn't leave. Then I remembered that the kids needed to feel loved and wanted. Maybe this would be the connection to family they needed. The doorbell rang at 5:20. I went to get it but no one else moved.

"Hi, you must be Lucy." I stuck my hand out in greeting, and she gave it a limp shake. I invited her in. Manny said hello and reached for his bag. Lucy looked around for Angel, who appeared at the top of the stairs.

"Come on, I don't have all day," Lucy said.

Angel took a step back. "I'll help you," I jumped in, trying to ease the tension. I climbed the stairs quickly making eye contact with Mike, imploring him to handle everyone else. He nodded once. Our friend stopped by to drop off art supplies as I reached Angel's room. I heard Mike explain what was happening and the neighbor's soft "Oh."

Lucy interjected, "She's coming with her real family."

Mike responded, "Yes, she's happy about that, Lucy."

Our friend offered the art supplies to Aunt Lucy and told her they were for Angel's art class. Lucy took them with surprise and said thank you. I lifted Angel's heavy bags and started for the stairs when she let out a little scream. I dropped the bag and turned toward her. "What is it?" I said in surprise.

"I'm not going! I'm not going, and you can't make me!"

I didn't know what to do. I tried to calm her. I was bewildered. Her screams rose, and her protest became firm. Lucy came up the stairs uninvited.

"That is enough!" she shouted. "Get in the car now, Angel." Angel wrapped her legs around her bed and gripped the footboard so tightly her knuckles turned white.

"Lucy, can I talk to her for a minute?" I asked cautiously.

Lucy stormed out of the room. Mike gathered the little kids up and took them in the backyard. Our friend volunteered to sit with them outside to avoid the commotion, and Mike agreed.

Meanwhile, Manny disappeared. Lucy was standing in the hallway on the phone with the police. I could hear her saying "They have my niece and nephew, and they won't give them back." She gave the address.

I left Angel's side and stepped into the hallway. "What are you doing?" I hissed. "She's just afraid."

That was the wrong thing to say. Lucy shouted back, "Oh, now they are afraid of me? You think you're so great because you're rich. I'm their blood. You're nothing."

I filled with rage and forgot all about keeping my cool. "I'm the one who was there for them. Where were you?"

Mike took the stairs two at a time and got to the top in time to get my attention. "Stop, Kristin. This isn't worth it. We can't do anything about this."

Angel continued screaming and cursing from the other room. The police showed up quickly. They knocked loudly and then entered following the sound of the disruption. Mike explained quietly what was going on. The officer took our identification and called DCS to confirm that Lucy was supposed to take the kids. Another officer entered Angel's room and talked calmly to her. I stepped back out and went to find my little kids. They were sitting on the back steps softly sobbing while our friend tried to distract them with a game of I spy. I hugged each of them and went back inside.

The officer was walking Angel down the stairs. Lucy was already in the car with the engine running.

"Manny's gone," Mike said with worry in his voice. The police officer asked us if we could go find him before Lucy reported him as a runaway.

"Are you kidding?" I shouted without disguising the frustration in my voice.

The police officer turned to look at me with warning in his eyes. Mike volunteered to go find Manny. I paced the family room in frustration. My friend stayed with the kids, and I was grateful. Mike and Manny returned 20 minutes later. Manny walked straight past the officers and his aunt and through the front door. He flung his arms around me and cried. I was stunned, tears pouring from me. Mike wrapped his arms around both of us.

A few minutes went by, and Manny untangled his arms and walked out the door. Mike and I watched through the front window as they drove away. I slid to the floor with my head in my hands, and Mike stood still for what felt like an eternity. Finally, I stood up, and Mike and I put our arms around each other, composing ourselves before retrieving our children from the back steps.

We didn't see Manny or Angel again for ten years.

Part 5

THE HOPE
OF SPRING

19

RELUCTANTLY OPEN

Grief consumed us. We decided to end our yearlong commitment early.

One week later, the phone rang.

I looked at the number on the screen and clicked the red button to decline the call and shoved the device back into my pocket.

The phone rang again. I pulled it back out of my pocket, glanced at the number, and said no. My finger hovered over the decline button once more, but instead, I silenced the ringer and placed the phone on the kitchen table and walked away. I took two steps and let out a sigh and turned back to see the glow of the persistent screen. "Fine," I said to no one as I punched accept. "Hello?" I said tentatively.

The caller cleared his throat. "Um, it's Frank. I should have called earlier. I'm sorry about how everything happened with Manny and Angel." He paused another moment before continuing, "I know you asked for some time, but I really need some help."

"We really can't right now," I interrupted. "We need a little bit to think things through." My words felt cold and determined.

"I know," he responded. "I wouldn't ask if it weren't really important, but I really need someone to take a little girl—tonight." I resisted the urge to interrupt him angrily. The desperation in his voice softened my resolve. I sank into my favorite armchair and reached for my notebook and pen. I took a deep breath and glanced at the clock—8:45 p.m. The kids were in bed, and Mike was watching a documentary that featured a different decade on each episode. He was on the '80s. He looked over at me and raised his eyebrows in question. I shrugged my shoulders, then urged Frank to continue.

"There is a five-year-old little girl here at the office right now. Another home came forward to take her little brothers, but they didn't feel equipped to take her. She's pretty difficult. Her house burned down tonight. Mom and Dad are both in the hospital, but the kids fared better. It looks like everyone will be fine—this is just an emergency placement. I don't have a lot of information for any of them right now, but I need you to know that this little girl is really struggling. She tried to bite me in the car." He paused again, and I could hear him take a deep breath. "Um, she also just urinated on herself. I have a coworker here who is helping her get changed. I understand if you can't do this right now. I really do. I just thought I would ask."

My firm resolve shattered. "Hang on," I said simply. I looked at Mike, who nodded his agreement. I didn't return to the call immediately but instead looked right at my partner, his eyes never leaving mine. I felt deep gratitude for his kind and generous heart and knew that in the days to come, I would want to cling to this moment of silent agreement, this moment where we again chose to jump into the unknown together. "Okay," I said to Frank, "we can take her."

He let out an audible breath. "Thank you, I will bring her to you in about 30 minutes, okay?" I agreed and hung up the phone.

Mike and I went to the guest room. It seemed so empty without Manny. We made the bed with a waterproof mattress protector and clean sheets. I dug the night-light out of a drawer in the bathroom.

Mike brought some of the girls' old clothes up from the basement. We kept various sizes just for occasions like this. I wasn't sure of hers, so I grabbed a few pairs of pants with adjustable waistbands, two dresses, and a cardigan with tiny embroidered flowers on the sleeve that Christine used to love. I held them to my chest for a moment to stir the memory of holding my girls when they were only five. Last, I pulled out one of Grace's favorite nightgowns and laid it on the bed for another small girl I had never met. I laid my hands on the items and silently prayed for a family struggling with heart-wrenching loss. I heard a faint knock at the door and felt grateful to Frank for realizing that the other kids were sleeping.

Mike answered it and pulled the door open to let Frank, his coworker, and a very small, wide-eyed little girl inside. Her hair struck me first, wild and curly and deep brown with one small silver streak in the front. My heart skipped a beat at the remembrance of another little girl, far in my past with a similar highlight. I crouched down to meet her eyes, and although the smell of smoke permeated the air, I decided we would do a bath only if she really felt up to it.

"Hello, I'm Kristin. I understand you've had a scary night. You are going to stay here tonight while your mommy and daddy visit the doctor." I reached my hand toward her.

Frank placed his hand on her back. "These people are safe. You will be safe. We can see your mom and dad tomorrow. Try to get some sleep, okay?"

She nodded but never took her eyes off the floor. We said good-bye and closed the door. Mike walked upstairs with us but left me to help her get into her pajamas. I cracked the door, always mindful of a child's need not to feel caged in with a stranger. I smiled and showed her the nightgown. She touched it but didn't say anything. "Do you need some help?" I asked, not knowing what to do.

She nodded again.

"Okay, here, let me pull your shirt over your head." She reached her arms up, and I pulled her shirt over her head, revealing insect bites all over her skin. I gasped and put my hand over my mouth. "Does that hurt?" She shrugged her shoulders. I asked her to turn around. Trails of bites marked every inch. "Bedbugs," I whispered. My heart started pounding. "Okay, this isn't a problem," I said. "We just need to do something to help your skin feel better. Come on, let's go to the bathroom."

I tried not to panic. I ran the bath and moved the little girl, whose name was Belle, into the steaming-hot tub. I poured bubble soap into the tub and let it run until bubbles threatened to spill onto the floor. I asked Mike to bring a plastic bag for her clothes. She slipped out of the clothes, and they fell in a pile at her feet. I scooped everything off the floor and into the bag, and Mike took the clothes to the laundry room and straight into the washer set on hot. Belle climbed into the tub as I dumped bath toys around her. She played quietly with a half-smile on her lips. I sprayed the floor with rubbing alcohol and then stepped out to spray the floor in the guest room where she had stood moments earlier. I opened a window to air out the smell and then moved to the hallway to catch my breath. I started to panic but talked myself down.

I thought the words were just in my head, but Christine opened her door a crack and asked, "Mommy, who are you talking to?"

I jumped. "Oh, honey, I'm sorry. I was talking to my brain."

Christine gestured to the bathroom. "Who is in there?"

I turned my head to check on Belle. She was still playing quietly in the tub, mesmerized by the bubbles, sticking one tiny finger into each shiny globe and laughing softly when it popped. "We have a little girl staying with us for a very short time. Her house burned down today, and she needed a place to stay." Christine looked at me thoughtfully for a moment and went back into her room. I thought she went back to bed, so I returned to the bathroom to begin the task of scrubbing this tiny stranger from head to foot.

Belle was relaxed in the bath, and helping her bathe wasn't difficult. Her tangled curls were another story. I grabbed a wide-toothed comb and, after lathering her hair with soap, I generously coated her head with conditioner. She peered up at me through long lashes, her hazel eyes taking on the color of the blue shower curtain for a moment. She simply shook her head.

"I'm sorry, Belle, I really have to comb this beautiful hair. You have some critters biting your skin, and that's not okay. I know you don't want me to, but I will be as gentle as possible." Her body tensed as she looked down at her bite-infested skin. She looked away from me but did not stop me. I took small sections of hair in between my thumb and forefinger and then combed from bottom to top. A few minutes later, I held the tangle-free section and admired my work. I smiled and showed Belle. She looked at it quickly and away again. I added more hot water and more conditioner over the next hour.

Finally, her hair was done. I rinsed her with fresh water, put the comb on the counter, and then grabbed the small mirror my girls kept there. I turned the mirror toward Belle. She turned her head side to side and admired her lovely hair. The water was getting cool, and Belle looked sleepy. I pulled a soft towel from the cabinet and gestured for her to get out. She shook her head. I held the towel up and asked her to get out. She shook her head again. She folded her arms in refusal. I yawned and covered my mouth with one end of the towel. She shook her head again, but the yawn was contagious, and she opened her little mouth in response. I stood there without a word, not wanting to enter a battle at this late hour.

She began to shiver. I moved a step closer with the towel still open. She relented and reached her arms toward me. I wrapped her in the soft terry cloth and dried her hair for a few minutes in front of the mirror. She watched as the steam disappeared. I wrapped her hair loosely in a bun and secured it with a soft hair tie. As I ran my fingers through her fine waves, I noticed a nearly microscopic bump. I moved her closer to the light and began to sift through her hair, silently praying I wouldn't find exactly what I knew I would find. Lice. My eyes closed shut, and I counted to ten before opening them.

I grabbed my phone and sent Frank a quick text to warn him to clean his car, office, and anything Belle touched while waiting for a family. I also asked him to let Belle's brothers' foster family know as well. He didn't respond, so I turned back to the situation unfolding in my bathroom. Exhausted, I decided to tackle the lice later. I retrieved an extra toothbrush from the linen closet and put a pea-sized dab of toothpaste on before handing it to Belle.

Mike had showered and changed his clothes while I completed the bath. He took over wiping the bathroom down and gathering items for the next load of laundry. I smiled at him with gratitude and promised to hug him once I had a chance to shower and change. He winked at me in response. Belle climbed into bed and found one of Christine's prized stuffed animals tucked between the sheets. My heart fluttered as I realized Christine's selfless act.

Belle hugged the stuffed lamb close to her as I tucked her in. She was asleep before I left the room. I hurried to the bathroom to scrub my own skin. I carefully stepped out of my clothes, placed them inside a plastic bag, tied it closed, and handed it to Mike to add to the wash. The water felt warm and comforting. I turned my face toward the spray and let the hot water wash over me.

Droplets hit my face, daring me to cry, and then I did. Tears escaped softly at first and then harder, ugly sobs. I cried for the little girl in the room next door. I wept for those who were so deeply missed and tears of gratitude for those we had met on this yearlong journey and the family I got to call my own every day. The water turned cold too quickly, and I stepped out of the spray. I dried my own hair and put it in a bun before slipping into warm sweats and a T-shirt. Mike was already asleep, and I could hear the soft hum of the washer and dryer in the basement as it lulled me to slumber.

Belle woke with a scream that shattered the peace. Grace, Christine, and Aaron were standing in the hallway with mouths agape by the time I ran to greet them. I quickly explained and asked them to go downstairs to start breakfast. I entered Belle's room and reminded her who I was and where she was. She slowly looked around and relaxed, but a single tear escaped, and she didn't bother to wipe it away. She was still clinging to the tiny lamb. I showed her some clean clothes, but she whispered, "I want my own clothes." She stuck her thumb in her mouth and looked away from me.

I wasn't sure how much to tell her about the extent of the fire, so I settled on telling her all that I knew. "We will see what we can find later today."

She accepted that answer and selected a pair of jeans, a glitter rainbow T-shirt, and a pale-yellow cardigan. The pants were huge on her, but they were the smallest I had. I cuffed the hem, cinched the waist, and stood back to see the result. "Pretty, just like your name," I told her, then patted her on the head. I remembered the lice and tried to cover cheerfully. "Okay, let's gather these sheets and put them in the wash." She reluctantly let go of the lamb, but I promised he was just having a bath and would be back soon. Belle and I walked down to the kitchen for breakfast and found that Mike had been to the grocery early before work and picked up lice treatment.

"Well, if that isn't true love, I don't know what is," I said with a laugh. My confused children just stared at me, and I waved the comment away with a dismissive gesture.

Once breakfast was over, I started the lice treatment on Belle's hair. The kids were home from school for a teachers' work day and wanted to go to the park. I checked the time—it was still early and barely light outside. I promised to take them after Belle's treatment. She was less than thrilled about having her hair covered in smelly gel and even less enthusiastic about holding her head over the kitchen sink while I combed the solution through her already tangled curls.

Grace scooted up on the counter next to her and told her all about how she hated having her curly hair shampooed too. She told her that she was pretty sure other moms were gentle but that I am the worst. She chattered on and on until I gave her a look of frustration. She rolled her eyes at me but changed her story by telling Belle that I'm probably not the worst, only maybe the second or third worst. I sighed but smiled despite myself. Grace scooted off the counter and went to her room to get changed for the day.

Aaron picked a movie for Belle and settled down in his favorite spot to watch. Belle was mesmerized by the Barbie princess movie, but I thought I might die if I had to watch the whole thing. Grace and Christine came skipping into the family room and settled down to watch. My suggestions for a different movie fell on deaf ears, and I relented and settled in as well. Turning my reading lamp toward Belle's head, I began to pull nits from the roots down to the end of each wavy strand. It was painstaking work, and my eyes hurt before I was halfway done. I realized I wouldn't make it through her whole head during the length of the movie, so I decided to stop halfway. I parted her hair down the middle and pulled it into two pigtails. Then I wrapped a scarf on her head and tried to pass it off as an accessory.

The kids were ready for a day at the park. They buckled into the car with such speed, my head began to spin. Belle climbed into the van awkwardly. She hadn't said much all morning. My heart hurt for her. She fit nicely into Grace's old booster. I was glad we kept it in the garage with easy access. The day was warm and sunny, trees were blooming all around, and the sweet smell of spring filled my senses. We drove to the park with all the windows down. It was a welcome relief after the last 12 hours of battling the pests that plagued Belle.

I was nervous about her touching the car and the house. I worried about the danger of infesting our family. As I drove, anger began to rise in me. I resented the foster-care system for asking me to do this again. I even began to feel angry toward Belle. I knew it was wrong, but thoughts of the unfairness of it all kept creeping back into my mind. I tried to shake them off, but they crept back in. I drove with hands gripped on the wheel and thought about Manny and Angel. I thought about Juniper and her separation from her family. I felt mad about all of it—and then I felt guilty. I adjusted the rearview mirror to capture her wide eyes. I silently apologized to her for feeling selfish. For a moment, she looked at me, and I imagined that she forgave me.

We hiked all morning. The renewal of life around us filled me with a sense of wonder. The winter had been long and cold and at times darker than I had imagined possible, but here was the proof that death and loss are in fact the beginning of life. I was caught up in my own thoughts when I felt a hard tap on my back. "Tag, you're it, Mommy!" It was Aaron, and I simply could not resist a good game of tag. I took off running.

20

THE INVITATION TO COME INSIDE

Belle and her brothers were able to visit with Mom and Dad throughout the month of April. The fire that raged through their home was caused by a faulty electrical outlet. Their home was occupied by three generations and everything those three generations had ever owned. The children were on the radar of the Department of Child Services because of the hazardous living conditions. The health department had warned them to clean up for the past two years after complaints from neighbors. The children were loved by their parents, grandparents, aunts, and uncles; they were neglected only in cleanliness. Unfortunately, that lack of attention to the home led to a situation that left them homeless.

Their entry into foster care revealed that they were all covered in bug bites and infested with lice. It took a month of treatments to clear Belle of lice. The break from home gave Mom and Dad the chance to become free from their own infestation. They seemed to want to get the kids back and into a healthy environment, but they had never lived anywhere else. It was difficult for Dad to understand that the way they were living was dangerous for the kids. Mom and

Dad worked with DCS to find housing they could afford. It was their first time living alone, and they were very nervous about it. All their furniture had burned, which was a bitter blessing because the furniture was likely carrying bugs.

Dad contacted a local church to ask if anyone had extra furniture. The church responded by filling their home with nearly every item they would need. DCS allowed us to visit anytime, so Mike and I were able to help assemble a crib and hang curtains. It was a fresh start, and Mom was brimming with excitement and pride over her mismatched but tidy home.

During one of the visits, Belle was playing with a box of Barbies donated by a family from the church. She turned to her dad and asked, "Where are my toys, Daddy? Am I going to get them back soon?"

Dad smiled but turned away. As we were leaving the house, Dad pulled Mike aside. "Would you be able to get one of my boxes out of storage? It wasn't in the fire, and it was sealed so it won't have bugs. It's in the shed at my mom's house. I don't have a car, but I was thinking you could get it on your way home."

Mike agreed without giving it much thought. He told me the plan as I buckled Belle into the car. The house was only a few blocks away, and we were feeling filled with the joy of helping others. Mike pulled the address up on his phone, and I followed the directions. We turned down the narrow one-way road and saw the house right away. Situated on a corner street, we could see the damage from all sides. There was barely anything but the foundation left. I gasped when I saw it.

Belle saw it too. She stuck her thumb in her mouth and started to whimper. It hadn't occurred to us that revisiting the scene would be traumatic for Belle. I pulled the van as close to the curb as possible, and Mike opened the door. He gingerly stepped around singed items strewn about the yard. I wondered if those items had always been there or if the chaos was another result of fire damage. I suspected the yard was much like the house had been, the chaos and disarray overtaking everything.

Mike reached the shed and located the bin quickly. He held it away from his body—it was dirty but not filthy. He slid the box into the back of the van and closed the door quickly. Not wanting to further traumatize Belle, I pulled away from the spot quickly and headed for the highway and home. We saw a Dairy Queen as we pulled off the exit toward our house, and I knew just what we needed. Ice cream. Belle smiled as we entered the drive-through. There is just something universal about feeding bad feelings with sweet treats. We each ate our ice cream quickly as we made the short trip from the restaurant to home. The month of May was sunny and warm, and the cool creaminess seemed fitting and welcome.

Our babysitter was in the backyard, playing with the other three kids. "How was your date night?" she asked jokingly.

"Oh, you know, very romantic," we responded, gesturing to the sticky five-year-old in the back seat and then to our work clothes. She laughed.

Our kids ran to the car, asking Belle all about her new house, and then frowned when they realized they had missed a trip to get ice cream. I promised we would go very soon, especially since we had received a good report from the babysitter. They cheered. Belle went into the backyard to play with the kids while we paid the sitter and waved goodbye.

Remembering the tote in the back of the car, I removed it and placed it on the driveway. Something uneasy came over me. "Maybe we should check it before we put it in the garage," I suggested. Mike agreed, and I lifted the lid. It was filled with old toys that belonged to the kids' father. I could see why he wanted it. I lifted the action figures and placed them on the driveway, revealing old VHS tapes in the bottom. Mike looked over my shoulder, and we laughed at the titles to old comedies.

We reminisced until we started to pack the items back in the tote and a cockroach crawled out of the inside of one of the movie cases down my forearm toward my elbow. I screamed. (I may have also said a curse word—my family will neither confirm nor deny this). I dropped the items into the tote and began laughing and crying at the same time. Shivers ran through my spine, and I suddenly felt phantom roaches were all over my skin. Another glance into the box revealed that it was swarming with recently disturbed roaches. They were streaming down the sides of the tub, crawling over one another to find an undisturbed place to hide. Mike stepped back and watched the scene, laughing but refusing to step forward to help.

"Thanks a lot!" I said in mock anger. He just shook his head at me. The kids ran to the driveway to see what was happening. I shouted for them to stay back. I picked up each thing with my thumb and forefinger to return it to the tote. "What are we going to do about the car?" I asked Mike.

"I don't know." He and I both felt overwhelmed.

"Okay, we'll put all of this in a large trash bag and leave it here on the lawn until I figure out what to do," I said. Mike grabbed a lawn-size garbage bag from the garage and held it while I lifted the tote inside. I tied it tightly and drug it to a far corner of our property. Then I shook my shirtsleeves and pant legs, hoping not to find any more critters inside.

We ushered the kids inside the house and put a movie on for them in the family room. Mike and I left our shoes outside and quickly went upstairs to shower and change. Once again, we wrapped our clothes in trash bags and took them to wash on the extra hot setting.

I went to the internet to find the best way to rid our home and car of any potential insect infestation.

Mike stayed with the kids while I drove to the grocery store to buy bug bombs. Normally I was afraid of using any poison around my kids, but this time, I would have used a real bomb on the car if it meant never seeing another roach again. I needed the time alone to collect myself and drove Mike's car instead of the van. Thirty minutes of browsing the insect repellant isle of the store did nothing to calm my fears.

I returned home to a quiet house. All the kids were in bed. I hated missing bedtime, but I had bigger fish to fry. I slipped into a pair of gardening gloves and went toward the van, ready for battle. I set two of the bug bombs off in the car and quickly closed the doors. I went inside to scrub my hands and do an assessment of my body once more to make sure there wasn't a bug near me. Thankfully there wasn't. I took one more shower, and once I felt squeaky clean, I went to my children's rooms to tuck them in. Belle was last. She was already sound asleep, snuggling her stuffed lamb close to her body. I smiled at her peaceful face. "You are worth it," I said. "You are worth everything." She rolled over and without opening her eyes, she smiled.

We weren't the only ones who noticed the lack of understanding about the dangers of having the house infested with roaches. We talked to Dad about the tote, but he seemed unconcerned. We hated to report the incident to DCS but felt we had no choice. Thankfully, they already knew.

Two weeks into May, when the kids were about to return home, we held a team meeting in the parent's family room. The home had been approved, and parent education was well underway. The room was packed with team members, two caseworkers, two sets of foster parents, a parent coach, a visit supervisor, one developmental therapist per child, a wraparound coordinator, the family minister from their church, and one very rowdy puppy the parents brought home against the advice of everyone on the team.

Belle was sitting on my lap and then crawling from her mom's lap to Dad's. She was doing well, but her energy level was rising with the temperature in the packed room. I gently patted her head when she climbed back to me again. She reached up and put two sticky fingers on either side of my face and smiled. I regretted having given her a peanut butter sandwich. I excused both of us, and we went into the kitchen to wash up. Belle touched a sticky finger to the white wall and then another to the counter. She giggled as she left behind one sticky handprint after another.

I crouched down next to her and whispered no. She let loose with a scream that nearly shattered the windows. I scooped her up, placed her on the countertop, and reached for a paper towel. There were no paper towels. The caseworker entered the kitchen to see what was going on. Her look of suspicion sent a wave of fear through me. "She's fine—just sticky hands." I held Belle's hands up for proof. "She wiped them on the walls too." I pointed. "I can't find a paper towel or washcloths…do you mind?" I gestured toward the cabinet with my own strawberry-jam-covered finger.

With one arm on Belle's leg, I turned the water to warm and tested it, and then I helped her put her hands under the tap and rubbed them together. "Rub and scrub, rub and scrub, make our hands so clean," we sang together. Belle loved the water, and her tantrum was momentarily forgotten. The caseworker opened two more cabinet doors and a drawer with no luck. Mom came in finally to see what all the fuss was about.

"We have made a little mess," I said. "We're trying to clean up, but I can't find your washcloths or paper towels."

Mom froze for a second, and I noticed her eyes dart around. "They're in the wash."

I sensed her fear. "That's okay. No problem, right, Belle?" She smiled, and I showed her how to dry her hands waving them in the air. The caseworker opened the cabinet below the sink, still looking for paper towels and I suspected something else as well. Mom turned away, and I looked down in time to see dozens of roaches scurry into the back of the cabinet. I scooped Belle into my arms and distracted her by puffing my cheeks out and shaking my head back and forth in a mock effort to dry her hands more quickly.

Mom and the caseworker stayed behind. Belle and I sat back in our spot in the middle of the meeting. Belle climbed off my lap and next to her father. The meeting resumed when everyone was in their place, but the caseworker looked displeased. I couldn't blame her; if there were roaches again, were their bedbugs too? My skin crawled with the thought. The concern was brought up in the meeting, and Mom and Dad were ashamed. They admitted they noticed the roaches but didn't remember what they were supposed to do.

I drove home with Belle that night in complete silence. I think she sensed the discomfort too. Her return home was so close, but it felt like it was slipping away. We entered our garage and left our shoes by the back door. I sighed at Mike, who was cleaning the last bit of the dinner dishes.

"I'm going to need some plastic bags," I said without emotion.

"Again?" he questioned. I nodded and took Belle to the bathroom to run the tub. She happily slid beneath the bubbles and played quietly while I told Mike what had happened. I didn't know if there was anything more serious than roaches, but I didn't want to take any chances, and neither did DCS. Mike agreed.

Belle had grown accustomed to bath time and handed me the

comb and conditioner without complaint. I brushed through her thick waves and felt love wash over me. I loved her so much. I loved her mom too, and her dad, and the extended family we met on visits. I could tell that she was loved and that with support, she would always be cared for by people who thought the world of her.

The next day, we were notified that the children would stop visits in the home until it had been cleared by a professional. We also learned that Mom would not be able to visit with the children again until her hair was free of lice and nits. She had the same curly hair as Belle, and I shuddered to think of the effort it would take to be certain.

Later that afternoon, she called me. She was in tears, and it took a few minutes to decipher what she was saying. She had given herself the lice treatment twice and was combing through her hair but didn't even know what she was looking for. She asked if I could come over and help. I selfishly started to tell her I couldn't possibly...I was just too busy. Then Belle came around the corner and into the kitchen. She was clutching the lamb that Christine had given her.

"Mama?" she questioned, pointing to the phone.

I nodded and covered the receiver, muffling my own voice. "Give me just a second, okay? I need to talk to Mama, and then I'll let you have a turn."

She complied, and I removed my hand before answering, "I can be there at eight thirty tonight. I just have to get the kids tucked into bed." Mom sniffled and thanked me. "It's okay," I responded. "Belle needs you to get through this. She needs you." I hung up and called Mike at work to let him know the plan.

That night, I tucked the kids in bed and put my hair up in a ponytail. I had become much less squeamish over the last few weeks when it came to bugs, but I was still cautious about bringing them home with me. When I arrived at the home, Mom was already in a T-shirt and sweats. She produced one more bottle of Nix lice treatment and the comb had I asked her to purchase. The apartment was cleaner than the last time, and I noticed right away that there were paper towels, sponges, and a bottle of multipurpose cleaner on the counter. I realized as I looked around that I felt connected to this mother. She was so different from me but still so similar—just a mom trying to figure out motherhood. I knew the feeling and told her so.

"Things are looking great around here. You are going to do just fine—the kids will be home before you know it." She smiled quickly and looked away in embarrassment. "Okay then, let's get to it!" I adjusted the temperature of the water, tested it with my hand, and asked her to do the same. She nodded, and I began to scrub her hair with the smelly shampoo. When we were done, we moved to the living room.

She gestured to the couch. "I vacuumed it so you won't get lice too." I nodded and sat down, tucking my knees under me so I could reach the top of her head while she sat cross-legged on the floor. I sectioned small chunks of hair with the back of the fine-toothed comb. I squeezed gel onto her scalp and pulled it through her hair, creating a slippery path to pinch and pull the tiny eggs from the root. She turned on the television and began to watch episodes of *The Office*. We laughed until our sides hurt as I brushed and pulled and wiped the comb. The previous awkwardness of the situation fell away—we could have been sisters or friends playing beauty salon. Sometime after midnight, her hair was complete. We both felt confident that the lice situation was behind us.

DCS required Mom and Dad to have a doctor's note stating they were free of lice and nits. They required them to have a signed paper from the landlord stating that the home was pest-free. I understood

the necessity of such documentation, but I imagined the embarrassment that Mom and Dad must be feeling.

As May neared its end, all the documentation was turned in to
their caseworker. The home was ready, and even as my love for Belle
grew, I knew her place was at home with her mom and dad. On
June 1, the order came in from the court to start a trial in-home visit.
Mike, Christine, Grace, Aaron, and I gathered Belle's things and
packed them into the van. We decided to drive her home together,
and the caseworker agreed that it would be the most logical transition for Belle.

Belle's brothers were already there when we climbed the steps to
the front porch. We could hear their laughter through the screen
door. Belle knocked politely, and Mom opened the door wide to
let her child come home. Belle ran inside, and the door swung shut
with a bang. We stood on the porch, not quite knowing what to do.

Our year of keeping our doors open was over. We were changed
and shaped in ways we never thought possible. Parts of us were
sharper, acutely aware of the hurt and loss within humanity. The
sharpness, however, stood in stark contrast to a new softness within
us. An awareness of our own faults and shortcomings that led to a
type of grace and love for others we never knew possible. The five
of us stood there looking at that closed screen door, listening to
the sounds of laughter and love inside, and Aaron started to cry.
Just then the screen door swung open once again, and there stood
Belle's mom, one arm holding the door wide and the other gesturing toward us.

"Come inside," she said. And we did.

ABOUT THE AUTHOR

Kristin Berry and her husband, Mike, are adoptive parents and former foster parents. They are cocreators of the award-winning blog *confessionsofanadoptiveparent.com*, which has more than 100,000 followers monthly and was named number three in the Top 100 Foster Blogs on the Planet in 2017 by Feedspot. It was also named one of the Top Adoptive Mom Blogs in 2016. Their podcast, *Honestly Adoption*, has more than 60,000 subscribers.

Mike and Kristin speak throughout the United States every year with a passion to reach overwhelmed foster and adoptive parents with a message of hope and camaraderie. They are the authors of several books, including *The Adoptive Parent Toolbox*, *The Weary Parent's Guide to Escaping Exhaustion*, *Confessions of an Adoptive Parent*, and *Honestly Adoption*. Mike is a featured writer on Disney's *Babble.com* and on *The Good Men Project*. His work has also appeared on *Yahoo Parent*, *Your Tango*, *Huffington Post*, *MichaelHyatt.com* and *Goinswriter.com*.

Mike and Kristin have been married 18 years and have eight children, all of whom are adopted. They reside in a suburb of Indianapolis, Indiana.

More Great Harvest House Books by Mike and Kristin Berry

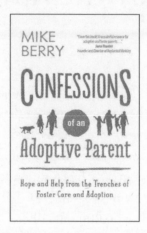

You Are Not Alone on This Journey

Adopting or fostering a child brings its own unique set of challenges only another parent facing the same uphill climb could possibly understand. From parenting children with traumatic pasts, to dealing with attachment issues, to raising a child with special needs, it can sometimes be a struggle just getting through the day.

Mike Berry knows the loneliness and isolation you can easily feel in your parenting role—because he's been there. He's *still there*, and he wants to give you the hope and encouragement you so desperately need.

There are plenty of how-to guides out there on parenting, but this one-of-a-kind book is specifically designed to address your needs as a parent of an adopted or foster child. With a refreshing dose of honesty, empathy, and care, you'll discover you are definitely not alone on your journey and God has a very special plan for you and your family.

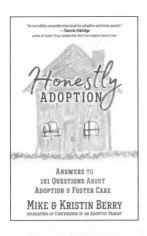

Discover What Adoption and Foster Care *Really* Look Like

If you are considering adoption or foster care or are already somewhere in this difficult and complicated process, you need trusted information from people who have been where you are.

Mike and Kristin Berry have adopted eight children and cared for another 23 kids in their nine-year stint as foster parents. They aren't just experts. They have experienced every emotional high and low and encountered virtually every situation imaginable as parents. Now, they want to share what they've learned with you.

Get the answers you need to the following questions, and many more:

Should I foster parent or adopt? How do I know?

What is the first step in becoming an adoptive or foster parent?

What are the benefits of an open versus closed adoption?

How and when do I tell my child that he or she is adopted?

How do I help my child embrace his or her cultural and racial identity?

Honestly Adoption will provide you with practical, down-to-earth advice to make good decisions in your own adoption and foster parenting journey and give you the help and hope you need.

To learn more about Harvest House books and
to read sample chapters, visit our website:

www.harvesthousepublishers.com

HARVEST HOUSE PUBLISHERS
EUGENE, OREGON